Aftermath
In the Wake of Murder

Carrie M. Freitag, MPS

AND

Margaret J. Kerouac, MS/CAS, CASAC, CCDC
Contributing Editor / Counseling Consultant

CHEVRON
PUBLISHING CORPORATION

Printed in the United States of America

ISBN: 1-883581-35-4

CHEVRON

PUBLISHING CORPORATION
5018 Dorsey Hall Drive, Suite 104
Ellicott City, MD 21042
410-740-0065

In Honor and Remembrance

This book is dedicated to...

My brother, William Freitag; all whose lives have been prematurely taken by violence; and all the survivors of murder victims who have shared their stories, their tears, and their strength so generously with me. I want you to know that the meaning of your loved ones' lives and deaths have not been wasted on me. I hope this book will serve as a testament to how important and unbelievably special their lives were.

My mother, Bev Freitag, who came to live with me after her son and home of 30 years had been set ablaze. We saw each other through the hardest years of our lives.

Daniel Leubner and Michael Taylor who saved my mother and a family friend from dying in the fire. They crawled into a burning house soaked with accelerant in an attempt to save my brother.

Howard "Lee" Cansler, a family friend and farmhand, who crawled over the roof of the burning house in an attempt to rescue my brother.

Firefighters at Mottville Voluntary Fire Department headed by Chief Ted Murdick and all the fire units responding from surrounding areas. They risked their lives trying to save our home and my brother.

NY State Police Investigator Aaron Roberts who carried on a persistent investigation despite the challenges and frustrations of the case.

Prosecutors Glen Suddaby and Tim Hennigan who were the gravitating force pulling together the 20-month investigation that resulted in the conviction of a dangerous man.

Although this book speaks to many disappointments regarding how our society responds to violence, it also honors the many heroes whose extraordinary efforts to help others serve as shining beacons of humanity that prevent murderous acts of evil from overshadowing the good that exists in people.

William Herbert Freitag
10/14/69-12/18/98

The youngest of four children, Bill grew up on the Freitag family farm in Skaneateles, NY, and lived there his entire life. He essentially started his career in farming and business before he started kindergarten. From the age of 3 or 4, he went out into the fields to work with his parents and siblings and charmed customers at the family's roadside vegetable stand. He loved nurturing relationships with both people and nature. Billy was dedicated to caring for the farm, growing the family business, and being there for his parents into their old age. Billy had a strong sense of obligation and responsibility. Many people's lives and futures were closely intertwined with his.

As a young adult, Bill expanded the family business to include flowers, fruit, vegetables, pumpkins, and Christmas trees—essentially turning a one-season market into a three-season market. He also had his own business, Freitag's Landscaping and Home Improvement, that included carpentry, landscaping, seawalls, patios, and home improvement.

From Christmas to Valentine's Day of each year, Billy would travel the country in his RV. He usually headed out with very little money in his pocket and made his living by doing odd jobs. Along the way, he communed with people from all walks of life, including outcasts and homeless people. Billy often turned strangers into friends. Each year, he would return to the farm with new stories and inspirations to share.

Bill believed in backing his values with both words and action. Billy poured his sweat, his creativity, his love, and his values into the way he lived his life. He played hard, worked hard, loved hard, dreamed big, and ventured further than most. He was willing to go to extraordinary lengths to help his friends. He brought life and meaning to concepts like compassion, generosity, honesty, loyalty, trust, faith, brotherhood, unconditional love, forgiveness, and freedom.

Unfortunately, he extended these gifts to one too many. A man who had been his friend for 20 years used Billy's identity to smuggle drugs into the country. This man was caught, arrested, and released on bail under Bill's name. While out on bail, he set Bill and the Freitags' home on fire. His motive was to deceive authorities into believing that the man they arrested for drug trafficking had died in an accidental house fire, thereby eliminating any chance of being held accountable for impersonation and drug trafficking. On Sept. 1, 2000, Billy's murderer was convicted of murder, arson, and criminal impersonation. He was sentenced to 25 years to life in prison.

Although Billy's last moments on earth were horrific, may we hold onto the light of his life instead of the darkness of his murder.

Table of Contents

Acknowledgements

The writing of this book was not a lone effort. As with all creative expressions, the words did not come from me, but through me. The words in this book echo the pleas and prayers of every murder victim survivor I have spoken to and corresponded with since my own brother was murdered on December 18, 1998. The words in this book echo the words of friends who knew the right things to say. The words in this book echo the gifts of faith, compassion, and wisdom that can evolve from profound tragedy.

I want to extend a special thank you to my contributing editor, Margaret "Peggy" Kerouac, MS/CAS, CASAC, CCDC, who has done everything in her power to help this book come to fruition. She has served as my front line editor, the one who stays up half the night polishing rocks to jewels. She has contributed her insights and creativity generously and humbly to this work drawing upon her expertise in mental health and human nature. Her faith and enthusiasm have fueled this project when my own inspiration was running low.

Another special thanks is due to my fellow murder victim survivor, Harry Hartman, who has read every chapter and boldly, honestly, and generously shared his reactions to this work and contributed his gifts of experience and wisdom. Harry has encouraged me daily to continue with this project. When I first asked Harry if he would be willing to read what I had completed of this book to help pierce the tunnel vision that sometimes traps writers, we were both part of an online support network of murder victim survivors. By the time I ended this project, we adopted one another as brothers and sisters in healing.

Foreword

By Margaret Kerouac

Murder affects everyone. No matter how many times we say "Not me, not my family, not my town, or not my community," our denial is shattered by the daily news. How close does murder have to strike to cause concern? How many murders have to occur before you make it your business to be knowledgeable about the subject? As you will discover by reading this book, one murder is too many and no one in society can afford to remain oblivious to the impact of murder on society at large.

An unequivocal response to murder occurred when the world watched the mass murders of Sept. 11, 2001. Over 3,000 people died as a result of four murderous groups. We all witnessed murder on the largest scale known in history on that day. Yet, the world still has to be sensitized to the fact that terrorism and murder have existed since the story of Cain and Abel. We have to wake up to the fact that we had more outrage for the loss of 3,000 people because their murders occurred the same day than we do for more than 18,000 murders per year in the United States alone. *Aftermath* helps us all to cope with the reality of murder on a case-by-case basis as well as on a mass scale. Granted, we did not see the other 18,000 murdered at once and we likely did not witness their murders on TV, but we have denied the impact of an average of 18,000 murders annually compared to 3,000 plus in a day. Although the impact was not seen on a mass scale, we can no longer respond to murder as if it is not a mass-scale problem—one murder at a time.

Carrie Freitag's brother, Bill, was murdered in 1998. The specifics about Bill's murder are covered in great detail in Carrie's second book, *White Flame* (in progress). *Aftermath* encompasses many murder scenarios as a result of Carrie's constant contact and work with other survivors of murder victims.

Her book started as a compilation of common discussion themes and advice shared in groups for survivors of murder victims. Her academic accomplishments including a master's degree in human services enabled her to encapsulate multiple components of murder and its aftermath in a single comprehensive resource tool.

Carrie's work started as a journal because she could not find books that met her needs on the subject of murder. Her journal notes were frequently shared and processed with other survivors, friends, and relatives. Carrie and I worked together extensively as I served in the capacity of counseling consultant and contributing editor for this book. We worked to create a resource as important to counseling professionals as it is to survivors.

The book is a wonderful blend of personal and professional material. Her research and personal experiences are masterfully interwoven with a creative writing style. The book is an easy read, yet a must read, because of the combination of compelling material and professionally relevant information.

Aftermath is a comprehensive guide for anyone seeking insight into human nature. Carrie Freitag has eloquently described the polar extremes of experiences that transpire when people are confronted with the best and worst in humans. If there is any way to offer comfort after a life-shattering trauma like murder of a loved one, then Carrie has captured the means in *Aftermath*. Just as the chapter titles indicate, she is able to dissect despair and convey hope, she can divulge grief and build faith. She can confront evil and hang on to goodness.

Aftermath is a must reference for anyone who has experienced loss—not just those affected by murder. However, the book is also specific to the needs of people surviving what is commonly referred to as complicated grief. Her book skillfully addresses matters specific to the special issues and obstacles of surviving murder victims.

When Carrie lost her brother, I feared losing all that was beautiful in her. She was gregarious, trusting, and pure of heart when I met her. I thought surely that person would die and would become another victim of the evil that could perpetuate murder. Instead, I watched her go through a complete metamorphosis. She moved out of the limited perspective of the caterpillar and up to the spiritual development and the perspective of a butterfly. She was forever transformed into an entirely new existence. The miracle was that she could be brutally honest with the horror and still come out a beautiful being. By capturing this transformation in a book, she is able to serve as a guide to all needing to rise above the cruel realities of our existence. She can help us all take the higher road when we are recovering from exposure to the worse evils our world has to offer.

The events of Sept. 11, 2001, made us all brutally aware that no one is excluded or safe from the impact of murder. The beauty of *Aftermath* is that we can rise up out of horror, transformed rather than damaged. We can learn to contend with evil without being consumed by evil. We all can develop skills to survive and avoid the pitfalls that serve to re-victimize the victim. Information, compassion, validation, and understanding are available. Whether you are trying to develop your own coping skills or trying to validate others, such as survivors of murder victims, then you must read this book.

About the Author and Contributing Editor

Celebrity Photo Shop, Baltimore

Carrie M. Freitag, MPS, grew up in the town of Skaneateles, NY, and graduated as salutatorian from Skaneateles High School in 1984. From there, she went to the University of Rochester where she graduated magna cum laude earning a Bachelor's degree with distinction in Health and Society and a minor in Biology. Carrie attended the Sloan Program in Health and Human Services Administration at Cornell University, graduating with a Master's degree in 1990. Currently, Carrie works as Senior Finance Manager for the Biomedical Engineering Department at Johns Hopkins University.

Since her brother's murder in 1998, Carrie has been immersed in the pursuit of justice; engaged almost daily in the mutual support of other murder victim survivors; and has participated in campaigns to block the parole of murderers, argue for maximum sentencing, and promote policies and decisions that hold violent criminals accountable for their actions and make our communities safer.

After her brother's murder, Carrie searched for reading material to help cope with the turmoil she was experiencing. The literature was sparse and inadequate. Most material spoke in sterile technical terms to mental health and criminal justice professionals without personally touching the hearts of those surviving the victims or those tangentially traumatized by murders in their community. Carrie wrote *Aftermath* to fill this void.

Margaret (Peggy) Kerouac, MS/CAS, CASAC, CCDC, served as counseling consultant and contributing editor to *Aftermath*. Peggy has 20 years of counseling experience and specializes in the areas of trauma recovery and addiction treatment.

Peggy grew up in Nashua, NH, and completed her undergraduate work at Norwich University, Northfield, VT. She was first licensed as Credentialed Alcoholism and Substance Abuse Counselor in New York in 1992. Peggy's Master degree and Certificate of Advance Study in Counseling were completed at the State University of New York at Oswego in 1996. Her graduate work, which earned the Lucy Wing Research Honors Award from SUNY, focused on treatment of adult survivors of incest and childhood sexual abuse.

Ms. Kerouac spent 15 years in upstate New York as a teacher and counselor. She worked at SUNY Oswego Counseling Center while completing her graduate work. She also operated a private counseling practice from 1994 to 1996. In 1996, she moved to Waycross, GA, to work as an instructor, general counselor, and guidance counselor for Waycross College. In 2000, Peggy joined the Job Corps staff as TEAP Counselor in Woodstock, MD. She runs several support groups for young adults, including a group for those who have suffered the loss of friends and family members to violence.

Darker Than Death

Every death brings to its survivors that one non-negotiable moment that hurts forever. That one moment, after which there is no returning home. Just as the dead have crossed a point of no return, those left behind to live cross a similar point when that first wave of grief divides everything we know into a before or an after. The waves of grief that follow remind us as dependably as the re-dawning of the sun that we cannot have what we miss the most. In an instant, life as we once knew it disappears and the future becomes a struggle between moving on and hanging on.

Survivors of all deaths are left to contend with this struggle and find a balance that allows them to emerge from their most pained and vulnerable moments with newfound strength and reasons for living. Although the struggle with grief is part of every death, murder is darker than death, and so is the road to surviving and healing in the aftermath. Murder devours innocent lives with a cruelty that is absent of reason, absent of values, and absent of compassion. Murder breaks all the sacred rules, knows no fairness, and can never be undone or compensated. It provokes fear and rage, and tempts us to battle it on its terms instead of ours. Murder drives even the most loving and compassionate people to the edge of that fine line that separates our respect for life from our violent potentials. The aftermath of murder takes us straight through hell where we stand eye-to-eye with the evil that hides behind human faces, and what we do in the face of that evil defines what lies behind our own face. The aftermath of murder is nothing less than a full-blown emotional and spiritual struggle.

In the struggle to re-establish a sense of peace, safety, and justice in our worlds, murder victim survivors find themselves contemplating everything from revenge to forgiveness. We are haunted by the existential questions. Why? Why like this? Where was God?

How can God or any higher power allow such cruelty and ugliness to prevail? Murder is a blow to the heart and a blow to the spirit. Murder tests our most fundamental beliefs. It is impossible to have a comprehensive discussion of death and murder without wandering into the realm of spiritual beliefs. Survivors of all faiths suffer in the aftermath of murder. Likewise, the support offered in this book is intended for people of all faiths. Although the divine name of God is spoken in many places throughout this book, the use of God's name is not meant to exclude.

When violence strikes, it hurts more than the victim. Its horror splashes onto everyone, the victim's family, friends, as well as the community. Murder renders useless most of the tools we normally use to cope with loss. Murder defies acceptance and reason. It violates and transforms almost every value and trust that once served to maintain a sense of peace and safety in our lives into a vulnerability that leaves us open to further loss and victimization. In the midst of this heightened vulnerability, the whole justice process demands that survivors relinquish control and establish trust at a time when their lives have just been violated in the most profound way by the ultimate betrayal to humanity—murder.

All too often, survivors struggle in solitude to assimilate the murder into their understanding of the world. We claw through the rubble looking for a foundation upon which to rebuild something that will both honor our loved one and withstand the horrors of the world. We live in a society that entertains itself with murder in books and on television, covers the topic relentlessly in the news every day, but remains relatively blind to the real struggle. Unfortunately, the reality of murder and the fiction of murder are often dangerously and painfully confused. Many people are not able to endure the discomfort of hearing what it is *really* like to have a loved one murdered without shutting down, changing the topic, offering shallow comforts, or making the survivor feel inappropriate for bringing it up or perhaps even flawed for not moving on with their lives more quickly.

Secondary wounds and betrayals are inflicted on top of the original loss by a criminal justice system that, by design, cares more about the rights of the criminal than the victim. The ineffectiveness and inefficiencies of our system prolong grief and seem to place our healing last on the agenda of an insufferable bureaucracy. Survivors are often gagged by the necessity of the criminal justice system to protect the integrity of evidence at a time when they most need to talk. Information regarding their loved one's death is often withheld when they most need to know, or revealed in the media when they most want to forget. Survivors must contend with the fear and anxiety that the murderer may someday live freely among us or already is living freely among us.

Aftermath is offered as a refuge to anyone who has lost a loved one at the wrongful hand of another, anyone who has been impacted by a murder in their community, or any person seeking insight into how we respond to violence as individuals and as a society. *Aftermath* offers a place for murder victim survivors to turn for validation, a place to discover that we are not as alone as we might feel. *Aftermath* pierces the isolation by lending words and images to free the experiences and feelings that lie mute in the hearts of far too many survivors. *Aftermath* also provides information regarding support networks and organizations where survivors can turn for additional information and assistance.

There is nothing in this book that will make the aftermath of murder easier to live through. Although this book is rich in validation and insight, the will to reclaim hope, faith, and all the things that make life worth living can only come from the individual survivor. Some words in this book may even trigger painful feelings and memories. *Aftermath* will honor the extreme challenges each survivor faces and cheerlead their way through the devastation. I encourage survivors to share this book with others and use it as a catalyst to communicate on a more meaningful level about how violence impacts us and how we find our way back to peace and happiness in the aftermath of murder.

Aftermath offers to you the words that I have most needed to hear since my own brother was murdered in December 1998. I can only hope that reading this book will help you as much as writing it has helped me.

CHAPTER ONE

Grief Is . . .

Grief is more than just a constellation of feelings in response to a loss. Grief does not fade with the passage of time. We do not realize our losses in an instant; we realize them over years. We do not get over it, but instead go through it, not just once, but as many times as we do. Through grief we honor our losses and weave them into the tapestries of our lives so we can stay connected with all we have loved and still continue to live on at the same time. We do not honor the dead with funerals alone; we honor them with our lives. Like love, grief is timeless. Like love, you cannot predict exactly how and when grief will manifest. Grief changes form and eludes definition.

Grief is physical. Grief sits on your chest, punches you in the gut, squeezes your throat, winds everything up breaking-point tight, and sucks the energy out of you. Grief is holding your breath, or breathing fast and shallow like a scared rabbit. Grief is lazy and lethargic. Grief is exhaustion that cannot sleep, hunger that cannot eat, and tears that will not dry. Grief makes you feel weak, hollow, and threadbare. Grief is clenching your teeth until you have a headache that will not go away. Grief is feeling rundown and getting sick over and over again. Grief is feeling so lousy all the time that you cannot tell whether you are sick or depressed.

Grief is a field of fog and distance where we wander lost and aimless. Grief is unexpected composure, lucidness, and productivity that seem out of place. Grief is rejecting the notion that someone is dead. Grief is a calm sullen silence, a vacuum into which we withdraw. Grief is forgetting and then remembering again that someone is really dead. Grief is not being able to think about anything else. Grief is dreaming about our loved one. Grief is feeling their presence, seeing their face, hearing their voice—even though they are dead—or being frustrated because we cannot.

Grief is a protest, a temper tantrum, a refusal to give up without a fight on something that is already gone. Grief is an intense negotiation over events that have already happened, a barrage of what-if's and if-only's. Grief is a hope turned backwards in time. Grief is yelling at the beautiful sunrise because it means time is abandoning your loved one. Grief is a plea to undo what cannot be undone. Grief is rejected offerings and ungranted prayers.

Grief is retracing the steps that led our loved one from this world. Grief is wanting to bear witness to and comfort the pain and suffering they experienced. Grief is feeling guilty because we did not stop death, could not prevent death, and cannot change death. Grief is an accountability session. Grief is damage control. Grief is knowing we do not deserve to be alive any more than our loved one deserves to be dead. Grief is wondering why fate chose them and not us. Grief is feeling guilty for moving on, guilty for living, and guilty for enjoying life without them. Is it irreverent to savor the foods they are no longer here to enjoy? Is it disrespectful to have a good belly laugh while mourning?

Grief is a sigh—a reluctant surrender to powers greater than us. Grief is a radical depletion of will and inspiration. Grief is throwing your hands up into the air and collapsing onto the floor in despair. Grief is unabashedly wailing and drowning in your own snot and tears. Grief is an inventory of what has been lost. Grief is a dim spotlight that illuminates the void where a life once was.

Grief is a fear that life is all there is and it is not enough. Grief is fear of living with the loss and fear of losing more. Grief clings to what we love as if every goodbye is the last. The imagination has a field day turning every early morning phone call into a death notice and every rush-hour delay into a fatal accident. Grief is examining every relationship, turning it upside down, considering its loss, and mourning it, before we venture to engage more deeply. Grief is choosing to endure loneliness and despair over facing the fear of further loss. Grief is coming to terms with the fact that we all will die someday whether we share life or experience it alone.

Grief is the identity crisis that ensues when we lose those who help define who we are, how we live, and how we relate to one another. And now that they are gone, are we still the person they helped define? How do we live? How do we relate? Certainly not the same. "How can I be a best friend if my best friend is dead?" "How can I be a big sister if my little brother is dead?" "How can I be a mother if I have no children left?" "How can I be a son after my father dies?" "What am I to be instead?" Grief is an influx of freedom to re-create the self as old expectations of who we once were fade. Grief is sometimes a vow to fulfill wishes of the dead.

Grief is panning through memories over and over searching for jewels. Grief is believing every pebble is a gem. Grief is a celebration. Grief is saying "thank you." Grief is admitting that there was no gold in the pan. Grief is a confession of regrets. Grief is saying "you are forgiven" or "forgive me." Grief is saying "God forgive you because I can't." Grief is saying "screw you for leaving me." Grief is turning ordinary objects—a hair brush, a note, a pin—into sacred vestiges. Grief is a moment frozen in time—a dead child's bedroom that will never be cleaned, a shirt that will never be washed, or a message on the answering machine that will never be erased. Grief is talking about your loved one again and again and choosing to ignore those that roll their eyes. Grief is avoiding the reminders and trying to forget. Grief is clinging to the reminders and trying to remember more. Grief is recalling special moments and crying. Grief is being able to remember the special moments and smiling instead of crying.

Grief is having a friend of your loved one pay a visit and realizing after they leave that there was more to your loved one than you ever knew. Grief is being inspired to carry out the acts of beauty and kindness that your love one is no longer here to deliver. Grief is buying lunch for the homeless man you normally ignore and sitting with him to eat because you know it is something your loved one would have done. Grief is understanding your loved one more by being more like them. Grief is understanding that you can still get to know someone better even after they are dead.

Grief is wondering where your loved one really is and if they can see you, hear you, or read your mind. Grief is waving or calling to them just in case. Grief is forging signs and symbols to replace the words you can no longer share. Grief is knowing the rainbow that should not scientifically exist on a cloudy day is a message to you saying "I exist." Grief is hearing that special song on the radio and knowing your loved one is with you. Grief is sitting in bed crying in the middle of the night saying "God, I miss you. Please, if you are there, give me sign" and hearing a bird sing a happy tune in the darkness and knowing that the song was your answer. Grief is discovering pieces of what was lost in places you do not expect. Grief is looking at the sunset and knowing it is extra beautiful because your loved one is a part of it and a part of creation greater than the scope of your contemplation.

Grief is grasping opportunities to connect, to share, and to care that you might have otherwise left for tomorrow because you are ever mindful now that there may be no tomorrow. Grief is being able to distinguish better what is really important and meaningful after all is said and done and choosing to do more of it. Grief is the yearning, the reaching, and the unrequited love that hides behind our losses. Grief is a tribute to the depth of your love.

CHAPTER TWO

Is There Peace In Knowing?

Death is intimate, a process ideally attended by our closest family and friends, who then share and describe those last moments to other loved ones who could not be there but wanted to be. Being present and knowing the details of our loved one's passing are both an honor and responsibility. With murder, there is nobody there to hold the victim's hand, bless their last breath, or tell them how much they are loved as they slip away from this world. The victim's last acts and last words are wasted on a heartless killer, and then strangers, such as policemen, paramedics, firemen, doctors, and medical examiners, swarm the scene. It can feel so very backwards and out-of-balance that strangers and murderers are privy to more about our loved one's death than the victim's surviving family members. The murderer steals not only a life, but also one of the most significant passages of a person's lifetime—death.

With murder, the truth is usually found in the details, strands upon strands of details just waiting to be woven into some semblance of truth and justice. Dealing with the details of the murder is one of the most difficult challenges a murder victim survivor has to face. "Should I visit the crime scene, the site of my loved one's death? Should I go to the morgue? Should I see the body? Should I run to their body, the broken and torn shell that once held their essence, or should I turn my head and look away? Should I seek out and talk with witnesses? Should I question my loved one's friends? Should I see the pictures and read the reports? Should I review the evidence? Should I sit in the courtroom at the trial? Should I, should I, should I?"

Wondering about our loved one's death is natural, not morbid. How were they murdered? How badly were they violated and brutalized? What were their last moments like? What were their last words? Were they scared? Did they fight? Did they suffer? Is there peace in knowing these details, or are we better off not knowing? I do not know. The unanswered questions can be just as heartbreaking and haunting as the answers.

Our imaginations reflect our fears as well as our wishes and place us on a pendulum of hope and horror. The facts and truths may slow the pendulum, but each detail and level of knowing introduces new dimensions of grief and outrage.

The reasons for wanting to know or choosing not to know are equally compelling. Being honest and realistic about what you can handle is critical. Knowing the details will not change what happened, so it really comes down to what role these details play for you in healing and restoring a sense of safety and justice in your world. Do not let anyone judge your decisions about wanting to know or not know the details. Others will always have opinions about what you should and should not see and hear. The first part of healing is learning to hear within yourself what it is you need to do and to regard your reasoning with compassion. Trust your intuition. Procrastinate and change your mind as often as you need to, and after you make a decision and act on it, do not turn back to beat up yourself with regrets no matter how horrible you feel. Someone you love has been murdered. You are going to feel horrible no matter how much you know about their death. Even when we are able to choose for ourselves what we are ready to see, hear, and know, we seldom really know whether we made the right choice. There is no easy path. The best you can do is explore your reasons for wanting to know or not know, consider your possible reactions, and make some reasoned choices.

While some survivors invest all of their resources and the rest of their lives into finding the answers that the police have not found or shared, others adopt a different philosophy. Knowing or not knowing, we are still left to cope with our powerlessness over both the manner and outcome of death. My child, my spouse, my sibling, my parent, will always be dead. Devoting one's life to figuring out the actions of a killer allows the murderer to siphon more resources and more energy from the living. Survivors, especially when the murder is unsolved, often fluctuate back and forth between the quest for the truth and resignation to the unknown.

Survivors sift through the details of their loved one's murder searching. Sometimes we are looking for a piece of our loved one, something to personalize and bring pride and dignity to their deaths, something amid the chaos and cruelty that the murderer could not steal, something that says, "Yes, he took my life, but not for a second did he take me." That "piece" might be finding out that your loved one's last moments were spent trying to save someone else's life or fighting to save their own. The detail could be learning that your little girl found it in her soul to look her rapist and murderer in the eye and say, "Jesus loves you" with her last breath. Sometimes we are searching for signs that our loved one did not suffer. "Please tell me that she was dead before she was dismembered." "Please tell me my 11-year-old son was killed first so he did not have to witness his older sister and father being slaughtered." "Please tell me my brother died before the flames touched his body."

Soldiers at war understand that peace can be found in the details and many make a point of sharing information about last days and moments with the families of their fallen comrades. "He fought hard and died quickly." "He was brave." "He brought hope and comfort to many in our platoon." "He had a good meal and a good laugh just moments before he died." Details like these, although difficult to hear, say more about the victim than the murderer and can help survivors reclaim a sense of dignity regarding their loved one's death.

Some survivors want to know all there is to know about the murder so they can retrace the steps that led their loved one from this world and bear witness to their suffering. In many ways learning what happened and how it happened can be the last act of caring and compassion we have to offer. Going through the pain of learning what happened to our loved one is a way of restoring some warmth and intimacy to their deaths, a way of showing them that we know and care about what happened to them. We are angry for them, sad for them, hurt for them, proud of them, and are there for them in their death just as we were there in their lives. "If I can stretch the arms of my empathy around the horror my brother endured and feel his fear and pain, then he has not died alone."

Although venturing through these feelings is a healthy, compassionate, and loving response, it can become an emotional trap. If we try to overcompensate for the time we missed and are missing with our loved one due to their premature death by obsessing with the negative details, we can find ourselves giving more meaning to their deaths than their lives. Your conscious mind was not meant to be used day in and day out as the master repository of information and emotions about your loved one's murder. You have to leave some energy and mental space for yourself and your life's missions too. Healing involves finding a balance between our feelings about our loved one's life *and* our feelings about their deaths. If it becomes all about death and murder all the time, we are in danger of stagnating in trauma and grief.

Nothing is more disheartening than being able to remember the murder scene more vividly than you remember your loved one's smile. The dark images can feel like a horrible desecration of something tender and precious. Turning away from pictures of our loved one lying in a pool of blood, hanging from a rope, crushed beneath the mangled wreck of a drunk driver, or lying in a fetal position charred to a crisp can be a way of preserving their dignity. Turning away from the details can be a way to honor the victim by preserving their image in their best moments—moments of smiling, laughter, and celebration of life. For some survivors, turning away from the details means never seeking them, for others it means choosing not to remember them, and for others it means trying to think about their loved one without thinking about the murder.

Sometimes we are willing to suffer the details so we can sit in the courtroom and support our loved one in their absence. You cannot go to any more baseball games, graduations, or weddings for your loved one, but you can be there to see justice done in their name. Unfortunately, in order to witness justice at work, you may have to endure something that is the emotional equivalent of attending your own child's stoning. We listen quietly as medical examiners explain in detail the physical damage and pain created by every injury inflicted upon our loved one. Often, we are hearing these things for the first time, with the jury, the judge, the media, and the defendant right there to witness our initial reactions. Nothing is more revolting and unnerving than to be sitting in the courtroom with your head down listening to the gruesome details of your loved one's death only to look up and catch the murderer enjoying your grief. Nothing is more demeaning than to have the defense make a motion to bar you from the courtroom because you cannot stop crying. Nothing is more awkward than having a television camera stuck in your face when you are still in shock from spending the day listening to how your loved one was brutalized. Although your presence in the courtroom is important, your composure and your well-being are extremely important too.

Ask the district attorney, the police, or a victim's advocate in advance of the trial to tell you as much as they can about the worst that you will hear in court so you can prepare yourself and your family emotionally. Most sensitive and creative professionals will find a way of phrasing things that will give you enough information to help you prepare yourself without jeopardizing the prosecution of the case. If they refuse, you can still prepare yourself for the possibilities by consulting forensic or medical texts to read about the pathology of various manners of death such as shootings, fire fatalities, or stabbings. If hearing the details is too hard, there is no shame in taking care of yourself and leaving the courtroom for parts of the testimony, if necessary.

Some survivors choose not to know the details to preserve their own mental health. The details and images of any murder are horrifying and traumatizing. Once known, the atrocities imbed themselves deeply into our internal landscape, prolonging and complicating our grief and posttraumatic reactions. You never forget. Dealing with the grief over the loss of a child, a parent, a sibling, or a friend, is more than enough to push most healthy individuals to the edge of their coping abilities. Sometimes our ability to function and make it through the day is all we have to hold on to and all we have to offer our family and friends that are still living. Getting out of bed, eating, sleeping, going to work, taking care of our bodies and homes— these basic functions are the bridge to healing. When these functions break down, things inevitably get worse before they get better. If letting in more details threatens to throw you off that bridge, it makes sense to wait until you reach the other side before taking on more. The murderer has already stolen one life, why let them have yours too? Choosing not to gamble with your mental health does not mean you are not strong, it means you are wise enough to know the limits of what you can handle.

Even when we make a decision to know the details, our minds find a way of steering us away from what we cannot handle through shock, dissociation, daydreaming, memory loss, sleep, etc. I remember sitting in the funeral director's office with my parents discussing arrangements for my brother's burnt body to be taken from the morgue to the crematory and his ashes returned to us. I kept waiting for the funeral director to offer us an opportunity to view the body, but the offer was never made, and I was afraid to ask. Afraid because the funeral director might think I was sick and morbid. Afraid because I did not think I could get the question out of my mouth without falling apart. It bothered me for months and years that I did not insist on seeing my brother's body. Did I not love him enough to insist on this? When I sought to do the next best thing, review the autopsy report and photos, I was denied access to everything because they were evidence in an open homicide case.

For two years, I kept asking the medical examiner, the district attorney, and the police to give me access to my brother's autopsy report and any information relating to my brother's death. I honestly believed I was ready to know the details regarding the condition of my brother's body and what that condition meant. I had read in fire investigation books what happens to human bodies in a fire and how the forensic evidence can provide information about the fire. Years before, unforeseen by me, I was incidentally prepped for this horror when I had assisted several autopsies on fire victims while doing an internship at the medical examiner's office during college. I knew what to expect and had considered the worst case scenario. Yet in the courtroom, when the medical examiner showed pictures of my brother's burnt face, three of us stood up and left. We all chose to walk away from the details for different reasons. One of us wanted to remember my brother's smiling face, not his burnt face. One of us was about to throw up. I left the room to resist the overwhelming urge to grab the murderer who was sitting 10 feet away by the back of the head and push his face into the picture of the burnt corpse screaming, "Look at what you did, you son of a bitch!"

After the trial when I was finally given a copy of the autopsy report, I sat with my most trusted friend to review it. Clearly after the first paragraph I could not read it aloud without choking up, so my friend took over. I woke up two hours later. To this day, I have not been able to stay awake to read or hear the details in their entirety. Sometimes our minds override our choices to protect us from what we are not ready to handle.

Others choose to avoid the gruesome details as a way of disempowering the murderer. Some murderers enjoy seeing others react to their heinous deed and knowing that they have violated even those that are still alive with fear and horror. Ignoring the details is one way of denying the murderer their sick satisfaction. It is very similar to discouraging a loud insulting obnoxious person by ignoring them. The less mental space we give up to the murderer's acts, the less power they have over us emotionally. The less we know about the murder and the murderer, the less reality there is to intrude into our thoughts and daily lives. This does not mean survivors choosing this route do not grieve and think about the murder, it just means that they try to keep their grief focused on their loved one by cleansing their thoughts of the vile, murderous acts.

Others choose not to know because they are afraid the details could strip them of their last remnants of self-restraint. They might fall off the edge of rage, hunt down the murderer to let them know what it feels like to suffer and die, or let them know that they cannot get away with killing *my* child, or *my* sister, or *my* mom. Seeing and knowing the details pierces any shred of denial that was insulating the survivor. Sometimes the details are so heinous and the victim so incredibly vulnerable that revenge can feel very right. Vengeance can even feel like the heroic thing to do. Fantasies of revenge are a normal part of grieving the murder of a loved one, but acting on these fantasies can only hurt the survivor more and further violate and distract us from the meaning of our loved one's life. If you act, the wrong person ends up in jail. Family members suffer yet another loss. Grief becomes compounded with regrets and shame. When the details are taunting you to violence and you fear you might lose control, it is okay to just walk away and choose to know no more. It is no different than walking away from a heated argument to preserve peace. Setting limits on how much of the murderer's sickness you are willing to absorb in order to understand what happened to your loved one is noble.

Often the circumstances of the murder place the victim at the center of a web of lies like suicides that are not suicides, accidents that are not accidents, or contrived circumstances out of character for the victim. Our efforts to learn exactly what happened can lead us to more deception and confusion than truth. This web is spun by the murderer to help evade detection and accountability, and also to defame and discredit the victim who is no longer alive to defend themselves. The un-knowing public is easily misinformed and the media runs with whatever information is available. The shelf life of news does not leave much time for verification. Survivors often bump head-on into the reality that nobody cares about the truth as much as they do and if they do not lead the pursuit of truth in their loved one's name, nobody will.

The pain of seeing your loved one's memory slandered can far outweigh the pain and anguish involved in sifting through the details of their murder to find the truth and make it known. Although voicing the truth is important, avoid getting derailed into a perpetual struggle with what the public is assuming, whispering, and concluding. Stay focused on what you know and what you need to know. If too much energy is devoted to verifying and arguing what others are saying, vital resources needed for your pursuit of truth, justice, and healing will be wasted. If the media is painting your loved one to be something other than what they were, the people that really matter, the ones who knew and cared about your loved one, will know the difference.

Sometimes the truth we desire is not the truth we find. Sometimes survivors discover that their loved one had a facet to their life that they kept secret. Sometimes we learn after a murder that our loved one was making poor judgments and engaging in risky or unsavory activities such as using drugs, partying too hard, having affairs, associating with dangerous people, etc. Suddenly the victim's life is under more scrutiny than the perpetrator's. Society justifies the horror of murder and the evil inside the murderer by focusing on the vulnerabilities and shortcomings of the victim to reap a false sense of security. "If he had chosen better friends, he would be alive today." "If only she had remembered not to talk to strangers." "If he hadn't been wandering around in a dangerous neighborhood." "If only she had gone home directly after school." "If she was not a prostitute, this would never have happened." The victim's flaws, shortcomings, and vulnerabilities *never* justify the murder, but their exploitation can intensify the loss. Murder is not the only type of death that reveals secrets. Under normal circumstances, secrets do not end up in headlines and do not become pivotal points in judging a life and death situation.

Sometimes the need to know has more to do with the pursuit of truth and justice than emotional needs. We are willing to do anything to assure that the murderer is caught and convicted, even if it means seeing and hearing horrifying details about how our loved one died. Evidence needs to be viewed relative to the victim's habits, lifestyle, and activities. Survivors are key to establishing what was normal for the victim. Building a profile of the victim is called victimology, and it is critical in helping investigators determine what among all the available pieces of evidence is significant. Consequently, survivors might be asked to view the victim's body, view the clothes they were wearing, view the possessions that were found on the person, look at photos, do a walk-through of the crime scene, and answer questions. Most murders involve people that know one another, so survivors may also have information that can help profile a suspect.

Unfortunately, the useful life of a crime scene is very short. The longer time elapses between the murder and the collection and documentation of evidence, the more easily compromised the evidence becomes in a court of law. Sometimes the circumstances demand that we expose ourselves to more than we are ready to handle emotionally, but we do it anyhow. Sometimes we have no choice but to swallow our hearts, pray for courage, and do the right thing. It is not uncommon for survivors to discover courage, composure, and dissociative skills they never knew they had.

Some survivors find themselves in the awkward situation of knowing a lot of very personal information about the victim's life. Often they are not comfortable sharing details such as affairs, drinking habits, sexual practices, drug addictions, use of prostitutes, sexual preferences, mood swings, or any behaviors and characteristics that might bias the police, the media, or the public against the victim. Answering the questions of investigators thoroughly and honestly can feel like a betrayal of your loved one, especially if the information you are disclosing does not seem pertinent to the murder case. On the other hand, if it later comes out that you omitted or concealed information, it can discredit all the information you did provide, jeopardize the case, and even place you under suspicion. Where do we draw the line between the victim's right to privacy and obstruction of justice? This is not an easy boundary to negotiate. A person is dead, and opening up their personal history for all to see can feel like throwing salt into profound wounds.

There are, however, a couple of hard rules to follow. Do not put anything into a written statement that is not true. Do not lie on the witness stand. If you feel a question is overly personal and not related to the case, say so, and take the time you need to decide what information you will provide. If it is really important, the question will be asked again. If it is really important, the investigators will try to explain why it is important to the case. If the defense discovers controversial information, they will likely use it to the murderer's advantage. By all means if you have sensitive information, share it with the district attorney so he or she can anticipate it being brought up and prepare for the disclosure. Sharing sensitive information gives the district attorney more opportunity for damage control and empowers them to diffuse inflammatory statements by the defense. Central to any defense is the attempt to shift focus from the defendant's actions and lifestyle to the victim's life choices. If you employ the "don't ask, don't tell" philosophy and choose not to share certain pieces of information with the police or district attorney, you should plan on being very careful with whom you do choose to share it. Do not jeopardize your own credibility, especially if there is a chance you will be called as a witness.

Some professionals understand the need that some survivors have to see and know all they can, and others simply do not get it. The trust that exists between the survivor, the investigators, and the district attorney can become a huge factor when dealing with issues of access to information. The investigators pick and choose what they share with survivors, and survivors pick and choose what information they share with them. We hope that somewhere in the middle the information comes together in a way that helps bring out the truth and bring about justice.

Investigators will hold back information from the family to minimize trauma and to protect the integrity of the evidence. Sometimes investigators hold back because they do not know if they can trust the survivors. Will they have a nervous breakdown right here in my office? Will the survivor try to beat police to the killer to carry out justice by themselves? Will the press exploit the survivor's naiveté and trick sensitive information out of them? Will one of the family members tell someone they trust, who tells someone they trust, and so on until the evidence gets watered down and washed away as hearsay in court? Will the information get back to someone who can jeopardize the investigation? Will vital clues get back to the suspect? Prosecutors and investigators have a lot to consider before they decide what to tell survivors, how to answer their questions, and how to gather evidence and information with discretion.

Once information about the murder is shared with you, you will also have to face these very same questions and dilemmas every time someone asks you about the murder. The knowledge can lead you to experience over and over the pain of telling and retelling the story. Assuming the role of the informer and the informed can be an overwhelming burden. Differing opinions about what should be known, who should know, what should be done with this knowledge, etc., can become a source of major conflict among surviving family members and friends. Some family members just want everyone to forget what happened and move on, while others want to keep digging and digging for more information. Some may believe that all information should be made public, while others believe that there are pieces that should be kept private. Some may want to involve the media while others will want to recite the "no comment" line the whole way.

Timing can be everything. Investigators use the information they have as leverage to get more information. The edge gets lost when too much information becomes too widely known, however once key witnesses have been interviewed and the suspect has been interrogated, the need to keep some pieces of information close to the chest might not be as important as it was before. Survivors might be ready to hear something a month or a year after the murder that they were not ready to hear in the days immediately following the murder. The trial converts sealed information into publicly available information. Having access to certain information before the trial could jeopardize the case, while access after the trial is relatively harmless. It can take years for a murder case to come to trial.

The process of investigation and prosecution limps along at the speed of bureaucratic sludge and doles out crumbs of information here and there. Just when we think we know the whole story, another crumb gets dropped. After the trial, we may encounter other barriers to getting information about our loved one's death. Transcripts for murder trials can cost thousands of dollars. Supposed public information is made financially inaccessible.

Unfortunately, circumstances often strip us of control over what information we have access to and how and when we are informed. Consider the mother who stops by to visit her son and finds him lying dead in a pool a coagulated blood with a trail of handprints and smears that tell of a struggle for life that carried through the whole house. She was not asked if she was ready to see the gore. Imagine the sister who has no means of confirming or dispelling rumors about her brother's body being surrounded by a satanic circle of candles because the police will not release any information until the case is tried. She was not given a choice about what she needed to know. Picture the family that after 10 years still has not been allowed to review the findings of their daughter's murder investigation because it is technically still an open case. They have not been given a choice. Think about the family members who were not allowed to sit in the courtroom because they were on the witness list, who were later told a copy of the trial transcript would cost them $5,000, and that arrangements for read-only access to the transcript could not be made. They are not being given a viable choice about what information they can access.

Being denied access to information that you believe you have a right to know can be frustrating and infuriating. After awhile it feels futile to throw question after question and lead after lead to the investigators, only to hear nothing back. Survivors are left feeling vulnerable and devalued when they are forced to get their information from the same newspapers, television stations, and rumor mills as the rest of the world. Being out of the loop can be even more frustrating when you have reason to believe the police are engaging in a cover up or are not thoroughly investigating the murder. The priority of your loved one's murder will never be as high to investigators as it is to you. Some investigators will go even further than withholding information, they will out and out lie to survivors to advance their own agenda. Since they have no obligation to disclose their investigative strategy or findings, there are no means available to evaluate the quality of their investigation and very little leverage to pressure them to do more. Survivors are left with a bellyful of worry that has no way of being validated or relieved. For some survivors, exclusion is permanent. The case is never solved. The records are never unsealed.

When and if you do learn the details, what do you do with them? It is not unusual for survivors to regret knowing what they do know, yet still long to know more. As I said before, there is no easy road. Survivors are often shocked by their own reactions to the details. Most survivors are traumatized in ways they cannot imagine when they visit the crime scene. Sometimes the scene does not even look like anything out of the ordinary happened. Clothes are still folded in neat piles. The dishes are still sitting in the sink waiting to be washed. How can everything that surrounded the murder look so normal when something so horrible has just happened?

Sometimes we expect to feel relief when we find out that our loved one died quickly, but instead find ourselves feeling twice as grief stricken. Why? Perhaps it is easier to ask a question than it is to grieve the answer. Even though the answer might be better or worse than what we feared, the bottom line is that our loved one is still dead. Each new piece of information blows fresh life into the horror and the loss. Sometimes our pursuit of facts distracts us from our grief. Sometimes we even subconsciously delude ourselves with the belief that when we finally put all the pieces of the puzzle together, we will find our loved one right there before our eyes. When we get all the pieces and our loved one does not appear, we enter a whole new level of grief that is centered more in our emotions than our intellect. The purpose is no longer about knowing, it is now about feeling.

What about those survivors that never know anything more about their loved one's murder than the fact that their loved one's dead body was found or that one day they simply did not come home? Typically there are only two people present for the actual murder—only two people who really know what happened—and one of them is dead and the other is untrustworthy. Beyond that, it is about piecing together evidence and inferring the truth. Some survivors spend the rest of their life digging and still never strike truth. Others know the truth, but the authorities cannot or have not collected the evidence needed to support the facts in a court of law. Even when you have been fully informed of the circumstances of the murder, there will always be some doubts and some blanks as to how exactly it happened. Try to use these blanks to bring yourself peace instead of torment.

These blanks are screens onto which we can project endless renditions of what the truth might be. The question I most want answered is, "What did my brother feel as he left this world?" I know he was doused with accelerant and set on fire in his sleep. I know he got up out of bed and died one arm's reach from a door that the murderer had jammed shut. I can guess, but try as I might, no matter how much information I have, I will never know for certain what he experienced. Perhaps I have experienced more of the details than he did. I will never know in my lifetime what pain God and the nature of human consciousness spared him. I will never know what was done to soothe his soul from his traumatic parting. I can fill my head with images of my brother's body sizzling and writhing in pain and his tortured face screaming for help that did not come, or I can picture him being wrapped in the ribbons of a rainbow and lifted from the fire by two doves. Neither image will ever change what happened. So what is the harm of taking my energy back from the images that bring me pain and channeling that energy into images that bring me peace? Which will honor my brother more? Wishful thinking or getting caught up in gruesome images that brew horror and rage?

It can be incredibly healing to separate ownership of the murder from ownership of the death. What your loved one experienced after their soul departed their body will always and forever belong to them and God—not the murderer. Ask yourself, whose soul do you believe was touched by the mercies of God and whose soul was stained by this evil act of murder? From a spiritual standpoint, the murderer is powerless to change the course of the victim's journey after they have passed from this world. The murder does not follow the victim through eternity, it follows the murderer.

CHAPTER THREE

Remembrance and Honor

People experience grief like the land experiences the ocean. Grief can come in tidal waves, gentle ripples, or hurricanes. Sometimes it is high tide. Sometimes it is low tide. Sometimes we take cover during grief storms, and other times we stand right in the middle of them, shouting back. We walk along the beach in the quiet aftermath, weathered and worn, picking up broken pieces and remnants of what was, trying to carry the driftwood of someone's lifetime in our arms as we continue reluctantly into the future.

Carrying the remnants of someone else's life in the forefront of our consciousness day-in and day-out is exhausting, but necessary for a time. We stop frequently and sit, turning the artifacts around and around in our hands, studying them, analyzing the meaning of our loved one's life and all we shared. Thirsty like a sponge, we try to soak up the meaning behind every little memory we carry, searching to feel our loved one's presence. We sense gusts of them over and over again as we play back time, but the memories are simply not enough to quench the thirsty heart of grief.

As ironic as it may sound, the key to carrying on without our loved one is not letting go of them, but rather figuring out how to stay connected to them after they are gone. How do we continue to live fully without leaving them behind? If we allow other people and other activities to occupy the space in our lives that once belonged solely to our deceased loved one, are we dishonoring them? The sun rises and falls while we live out the answers to these questions. Remembering and honoring the dead are lifelong spiritual and emotional missions. Sometimes remembering and honoring competes with living, but as we assimilate the meaning of our loved one's life and death into our own lives, we connect with them on a deeper level that enables us to set down the pieces of driftwood and run unencumbered along the beach once again.

Most survivors go through periods when they think about their murdered loved one almost constantly. Keeping them in your everyday consciousness is a way of assuring that memories stay fresh and alive. Remembrance and honor are a very important part of loving and grieving. It is healthy to devote this kind of energy to grief. Part of grieving is finding a place inside ourselves for all the memories, meanings, and gifts that our loved one left with us. By drawing upon these treasures throughout our own lives, we continue to know our loved one.

Many survivors find themselves lost and overwhelmed in a room so crowded with memories they cannot find the way out. We try to remember our way back home, back to something familiar. But where is home? Is it where my brother died? Where my mother lived? Where my baby is buried? In the photo albums on the shelf? The images that now make us cry instead of smile when we look at them? Even our memories do not feel familiar. The gravity is gone. We frantically try to hold onto every memory that crosses our mind for fear it will float away and be lost forever.

Experiencing memories over and over is part of appreciating the value of someone's life, which is one way of expressing gratitude for the gift of life in general. But, ruminating and obsessing are valuing the life of your loved one more than your own. Beholding special memories keeps us in touch with special places within ourselves that we once shared with our loved one. On the roller coaster of grief, these memories can feel like precious gifts one moment, only to turn into heartache the next. Our emotional reactions can fluctuate dramatically with every memory we visit, leaving us confused and conflicted inside. What once brought us happiness, now triggers sadness, anger, guilt, and longing. We want to remember, but it hurts. We want to forget, but it hurts. For a time, we are trapped. We remain stuck in the room of remembrance until we understand that we can leave the room, return, and leave again without getting stuck inside or outside of the room. As we learn to move freely in and out of the room of remembrance, the room becomes part of our emotional and spiritual home that goes with us everywhere we go. This assimilation happens over years—not days.

The pain and loss we feel when a life ends measure the depth and generosity of the gifts we shared. Grief has as much to do with what has been given as what has been lost. The pain of what is missing testifies to the gifts we enjoyed. When people die, they take a piece of everyone that ever loved them to heaven with them. Only through remembering and honoring the dead do we come to understand spiritually, intellectually, and emotionally that our losses and our gifts are one and the same. The losses that leave us crying here on earth may be the very gifts being rejoiced in heaven. Part of grieving is discovering that love is the only thing we take and leave in this world that matters. The rest is just a husk that is shed. Our love outlives our bodies. Our love outlives our wrongs. Love is spiritual, not physical. Love connects our souls across time and space. The love between souls is never really lost.

All lives are deserving of mourning, deserving of celebrating, deserving of remembering, and deserving of honoring long beyond the last breath taken. Remembrance has no timeclock. Do not stop remembering just because someone else believes you have grieved long enough. Honor and remembrance are your right and your loved one's right. There are a myriad of ways to remember and honor the dead. Each survivor eventually develops their own approach. We can remember and honor our loved one with tombstones, beautiful gardens, loving words, pictures, and prayers. We can honor them in our conversations with others. We can light a candle in the solitude of our own home or stand among hundreds of people in a candlelight vigil. We can post memorial ads in the newspaper or remember them in masses at church. We can remember them with pictures or sentimental objects. Survivors remember and honor their loved ones differently at different times. There are no rules to remembrance and honor.

There are many dates that bring us to remember and honor our loved one more than others, such as the victim's birthday, Mother's Day, Father's Day, Christmas, weddings, graduations, family reunions, anniversaries, etc. These special days will never feel the same as they once did. How do we celebrate our murdered child's birthday when they are not here to receive our gifts? How do we celebrate Mother's Day and Father's Day when the void of one less child on earth to say "Happy Mother's Day" or

"Happy Father's Day" looms large in our hearts? We may try our best to fill the day with happy moments, nice meals, a newly-planted garden, a bigger-than-usual hug, but each smile and each laugh is separated by the grief that cannot be ignored. While we may be happy for the gifts each of us brings to one another on these special days, we want most what we miss most, and that is something we are powerless to give one another. At best, we can be with our living family members and loved ones in the same spirit that we would want to share with our deceased loved one if they were here. We can hope and pray that somehow, someway, our deceased loved one will find a way to be with us; that we may feel their presence, and they feel ours, even if only for a few moments; and that we can end the day with our faith reaffirmed. Remembrance and honor are key ingredients to spiritually connecting with the dead.

Some survivors feel the year of "firsts" is the hardest—the first Christmas without our deceased loved one, the first birthday, the first Easter, etc. Others find the years that follow to be harder because the loss of yet another year is denoted. The timeclock of grief repeats itself. You do not mourn the loss of just one Christmas without your loved one. A year goes by, and you mourn the loss of two. A year goes by, and you mourn the loss of three. A year goes by, and you mourn the loss of four Christmases. Grief compounds over time. "My little girl would have been 16 this year and driving a car." "My son would have been 22 and graduating from college." "My husband would have walked his daughter down the aisle to the altar today." Our losses are realized over years and decades. The loss we deal with on these special days does not really diminish with time, but we change. We may become more accepting of what we cannot change. We may become more connected to the spiritual world. We may overcome loneliness by establishing new or deeper relationships. As we change, we experience our losses differently.

Some survivors may reach a point where they actually forget the victim's birthday or forget to light a candle for them on special holidays. This can be viewed with mixed feelings. Some consider it a sign of healing and re-engaging with life, while others consider it a horrible betrayal. Survivors may beat up themselves afterward because they equate forgetting a date with dishonoring their loved one. Do not punish yourself for remembering or not remembering when you think you should. The fact that you do remember your loved one is far more important than when. When my brother was alive, I did not think about him everyday like I do now, but I never forgot his birthday. Now that he is dead, I think of him everyday, birthday or not. I have even forgotten his birthday some years, but never once did I forget him.

The anniversary of the murder can be a significant day of honor, remembrance, and mourning—a day dreaded by many murder victim survivors. Survivors commonly find themselves plunged back into the emotional state they experienced when they first learned of their loved one's murder. Survivors may re-experience intrusive thoughts and images of the horror their loved one endured. All too often instead of feeling like a memorial to our loved one, the murder anniversary can feel like a re-victimization. Revisiting our loved one's death usually involves revisiting some or all aspects of the murder. Some survivors do not see the point of rehashing the horror. It feels like a defilement instead of a tribute, so they choose to let the day pass as unnoticed and unrecognized as possible. Some survivors learn to reclaim the day from the murderer. They stop calling it the anniversary of the murder and find something more special to name the day—the anniversary of my loved one's passing into the spiritual realm, the day my loved one was called home, or angel day.

Murder anniversaries can be awkward. People not as affected by the murder will not likely remember the exact date unless you tell them. Telling people that it is the anniversary of the murder can be enough to trigger the very emotional reactions in yourself that you wish to avoid. Yet if you do not tell people, they may not understand your behavior if you should have a hard time emotionally. It may be wise, especially in the first couple of years after the murder, to allow yourself the time and space to just "be" on this day—be sad, be hysterical, be solemn, be normal, be with whom you need to be with, and do whatever it is you need to do without having to worry about what others think or expect from you. Some survivors find that despite all the negative anticipation of the anniversary, they make it through day with such unexpected composure that they wonder why they put so much emotional weight on the day to begin with? Anniversaries are something we see coming and have a chance to "gear up" for. Some of us do so many dress rehearsals in our heads that when the day comes, the emotional energy has already been expended, allowing us unexpected calm.

Funerals are also filled with remembrance and honor. Many survivors are afraid to attend other people's funerals for some time after their loved one's murder. They fear that being around other people's "new grief" will trigger their "old grief" and that their presence will be more of a liability than a comfort to the newly bereaved. Survivors may fear that their emotional reactions will turn an event that is supposed to be dedicated to remembering and honoring someone else's life and death into something about their own losses.

It is impossible to attend the loss of another human being without revisiting the loss of others we have loved and without anticipating, on some level, what it would be like to lose yet another. We do not really experience just one loss at a time because one loss triggers the feelings about all the past losses, especially if there are unresolved feelings and issues. This is true whether we are talking about deaths, relationships that have ended, or other life changes that involve saying goodbye to someone or something. They all involve loss and grieving.

Ironically, when survivors do find the courage to attend a funeral again, many find it more healing and re-affirming than re-traumatizing. Survivors often discover new insight into their situation by participating in remembering, honoring, and mourning a natural death. Some discover that the meaning of their murdered loved one's life and passing was not diminished or amplified by their manner of death. Some discover new depths of compassion and empathy. Others discover that they still have more mourning to do. Others discover that they have mourned enough. Some discover that they are not as alone in their grief as they thought. Although it takes courage to help others through their losses, extending ourselves in this way opens the door to new gifts of wisdom, healing, and discovery.

Through remembrance and honor, we cultivate our continued

relationships with our deceased loved ones. Remembering and honoring involves more than merely recounting who our loved ones once were. Remembering and honoring involves recognizing their continued existence and continued importance in our hearts and in our lives. When our loved ones were in the physical world, all they knew of us was what we told them. Now that they are in the spiritual realm, we may develop the sense that they can see and know everything that is going on in our lives. When we have faith that they are still with us, it frees us to continue talking to and relating to them. So oddly, it is completely possible to feel as close or closer to our loved ones after they have died and passed beyond the limitations of the physical realm.

CHAPTER FOUR

Strangers In The Family

Murder breaches our connections with others suddenly and profoundly. We are instantly different than how we once were, changed in ways that may be difficult for others to understand or fully accept. Our emotional state is different. Our minds are preoccupied by different thoughts, questions, and priorities. Grief and trauma turn us into strangers even to ourselves.

Feeling lost and alone in the world after someone you love dies is not unusual. Feelings of isolation and loneliness are part of grieving. When our connections with someone important in our lives are abruptly severed, we are not only cut off from them, but also from parts of ourselves. All significant relationships have special aspects that are unique to the relationship and irreplaceable. A whole way of being is lost when someone close dies. The aspects of our lives from which we feel severed will vary depending upon who we have lost. Grief is different for each of us. "I'm grieving a brother, while you grieve a son." "I lost a wife, and you lost a mom." Even when grieving for the same person, we miss and ache for different aspects of them. We all grieve so differently and yet so painfully the same.

The murderer takes more than just one life. Murder has the potential of swallowing families and even entire communities. When someone is murdered, the family is confronted with issues that are foreign to them. We see parts of each other that perhaps we had never seen before. Family members that have *always* been there for us might withdraw emotionally or just give up. We might see episodes of rage reach proportions that we never thought the other person was capable of reaching. We may even witness strength, spiritual depth, and sensitivity that we did not know was there. Grief and rage transform each member of the family in their own way and in their own time. Some families go through phases when they are barely recognizable to one another.

The absence of one affects the dynamics of the whole and it is impossible for the family to ever be the same as it once was. When one is taken, a piece of everybody goes with them. The family does not fit together the same. The engine does not run the same. When the family finally musters the collective courage to sit for the next family portrait on the wall, the blank outline of who is not there stands clearly among them. Seeing our loss in its cumulative whole pushes our grief to new levels of intensity. Observing others grieve opens new dimensions to our own grief and unmasks the true magnitude of our pain.

Surviving family members may find themselves retreating from one another to escape the pain, ultimately intensifying their loneliness and intensifying their longing for what was. No matter how much we withdraw, there is no way to escape the pain when we see it in the eyes of our children or our spouse everytime they pass the empty bedroom. "I don't talk about my daughter's murder with my husband or her only surviving sibling. Even at the mention of my daughter's name, my husband starts crying or raging and his whole day is ruined. Anytime I mention the murder to my son, he tells me he is trying to get past it and prefers not to discuss it. So, my daughter's only three surviving relatives barely acknowledge her existence to one another even though each of us was profoundly impacted by her life and by her death." It is not uncommon for the victim's memory to be kept alive in the community, but within the victim's own household, their memory may be treated as if it were invisible.

Grief collides with grief and our varying means of coping become a source of alienation, friction, and pain. Seeing our family members grieve can hurt more than grieving ourselves. Grief can become ingrown upon the family. It may feel as if the family is simply too close to grieve without hurting one another. Sometimes no one is far enough out of the quicksand to pull the others out and efforts to help each other just entrench everyone deeper in feelings of despair, defeat, disappointment, and emotional exhaustion. Some family members end up becoming caretakers when what they really seek is comfort. Other family members end up crumbling every time they try to offer themselves as pillars of strength. Our expectations regarding "how we should deal with our loss" can transform our grief into guilt and resentment, especially when the family's emotional reserves are so depleted that nobody's needs are being met.

Family members sometimes get confused over whose grief is whose and blame their pain on other family members. "If only she could control her grief, I could control mine." But ultimately, the pain we feel, whether it is individually or as a family, *is* the pain that is ours to deal with. If we cannot handle our family members' grief, it is probably because we cannot handle our own. The only way to embrace someone else's loss is to first find the courage and compassion to embrace our own. We must take ownership for our own grief and take responsibility for finding ways to meet our own emotional needs so that we can learn to meet the emotional needs of those we love who are still living. When family members find the courage to embrace one another's pain instead of pushing it away, this horrible event that threatens to drive the family apart can actually bring it closer together.

When people grieve in different ways, it can be helpful to discuss how individual reactions to the murder are affecting one another and how to help each other grieve. Sometimes the best way to help each other is to admit to our inability to diminish one another's pain and simply allow one another the space to grieve. Although it can hurt to see others grieve, we learn to cope with grief faster if we can learn from the experiences of each other as well our own experiences. Try to be a model where you are at with your own grief rather than trying to fix where you think your family should be with their grief.

Space to grieve can mean many things. It means compassion, compromise, and understanding. It means accepting that others might not feel the same way as we do and respecting the right of others to feel whatever they feel. Space to grieve means recognizing that others hurt just as much as we do, even though different things may trigger their pain. Space to grieve may mean devoting specific times solely to remembering and talking about our loved one. Space to grieve means understanding that others might not be ready to partake in heavy conversations about grief and murder right now. Space to grieve may mean time alone. Or, it might literally mean physical space devoted to honoring and remembering our loved one, or physical space that is free of remembrances. Giving someone the space to grieve can even mean finding the courage to hold them while they cry, allowing them to grieve within our embrace even if it makes us cry too.

Space to grieve also can mean giving others the space to live. It is important to allow times when the family can talk without mentioning the murder of their loved one, or do things together that have nothing to do with murder, death, or mourning. Continue to encourage one another to live. If the family fails to balance grieving with living, family members, especially children, may come to feel devalued and alienated. "It seems that since my sister died, nothing I do excites my parents or makes them proud of me. They only want to talk about how great she was. They don't seem to care about anything I do." "The only way to get any attention in this family is to die." "Since my brother died, my parents act as if I am doing something wrong when I laugh, joke, and play. My brother was allowed to laugh when he was alive, and it makes me mad that it's no longer okay to laugh just because he is no longer here." If family members feel that they have to hide their joy and investment in living from one another, the family is destined to be destroyed by the murderer leaving even more devastation in the wake of murder.

Space to grieve means accepting the fact that everyone's needs cannot be met at once. It also means making an effort to understand what each other's needs are so that someday the family can find ways to comfort one another. We may not understand each other's reactions to the murder now, but someday we might. The sibling of a murder victim might not fully comprehend their parents' grief until they are grown and have children of their own. People do not pass through the phases of grief and trauma in the same order. One family member may be immersed in denial, while another is caught in rage, while still another is paralyzed with depression. It is always to our advantage to handle one another's reactions with as much thoughtfulness and sensitivity as we can muster. Our compassion with family members now may help us deal more compassionately with ourselves later should we enter phases of grief similar to what they are experiencing. The kind words of support we offer each other now may later become the very words we need to hear. If we withhold our comfort and understanding from each other, it makes it harder down the line to ask for or accept these same comforts for ourselves.

Sometimes survivors feel pained by the things that were not changed by the death of their loved one. Although it seems that such a sudden and violent loss should shock us all into good behavior, it is not realistic to expect the best behavior from anyone after the murder of a loved one. Families that were dysfunctional before the murder will typically be dysfunctional after the murder. The drinkers may still drink. The anorexics may still starve. The jealous may still be green. The ragers may still rage. The cheaters may still cheat. The addicts may still seek their fix. The deceitful may still deceive. And, the fighters may still fight. In fact, the murder may cause dysfunctions to escalate. All the old problems are still there and often become interwoven with new pain and crisis.

There is little room for behaviors that are going to test our patience, drain our energy, or twist our emotions when we are in the midst of the most stressful and painful time of our life. Some survivors find they are even more resentful of the failures of the family because they believe their deceased loved one deserved better. Now that they are dead, there is no hope for them to experience anything better than what they got. The circumstances demand of us the utmost compassion and understanding at a time when our tolerance and emotional resilience is running at an all-time low.

Our closeness with family and friends is in part measured by how much we can confide in them, how much we trust them with our vulnerabilities, and how much emotional energy we share with them. What does it mean if we choose to discuss the murder and seek emotional support from friends instead of family, or strangers instead of friends? Some survivors experience a nagging concern that the need to reach outside of the family for support somehow speaks negatively to the closeness and stability of the family. We may feel as if we are working through things with others that we should really be working through with our own family members. Seeking support from others outside the family does not equate to withdrawing from the family or abandoning the family. If your garden failed to produce enough food to feed your family, nobody would fault you for seeking food elsewhere. Seeking emotional support from those less impacted by the murder may simply be a way of better assuring that your emotional needs get met. This, in turn, will make it easier for you to see beyond your own needs and to begin to understand and respond to the needs of those who are closest to you.

Survivors may find themselves pondering what it would be like to lose other family members. We may find ourselves welling up with tears for people who have not even died yet—thanking God that they are still with us. As much as these are tears of grief, they are also tears of gratitude for the time that we still have with those we love. If we can emerge from the aftermath of murder hugging each other a little tighter, visiting with each other a little longer or more frequently, then we have grasped the gift of our loved one's parting. If nothing else, let the passing of our loved ones re-affirm just how precious life is and how short the leap from grief to gratitude can be.

CHAPTER FIVE

Feeling Alone in a World Full of People

Grief is the lone sojourn of wounded spirits trying to find their way back to wholeness. No matter how many people share our grief, no one can bear it for us. Grief is self-absorbing, sometimes leaving us blind, deaf, and mute to those that walk by our side. We walk alone until we find words to speak of our losses and room within our sorrow-laden hearts to embrace the losses that others have endured with us.

Some relationships bond with grief, other relationships dissipate in it, while others simply drown in it. The tug of war between isolation and our need to feel connected again is part of normal grieving. We experience aspects of this struggle with all our losses. Murder multiplies the dimensions of the conflict between the urge to isolate and the need to connect by throwing violence, trauma, betrayal, and questions of safety and justice into the equation.

In the aftermath of murder, betrayal is a common theme that weaves through the survivor's beliefs about humanity. We feel betrayed by the killer, betrayed by people who just are not there for us in the way we need them to be, or perhaps betrayed by law enforcement, the media, or the justice system itself. What if we have already reached for help that is supposed to be there and found it to be nothing more than a lie? Where do we turn then? How can we risk reaching out for human connection when it feels as if one more failure of humanity will be enough to sink what little faith in people remains.

Survivors sometimes feel betrayed by how others react or fail to react to the murder. It is natural to want others to feel as impassioned and outraged about the murder as we do. When the emotional stakes are high, tolerance for ambivalence, indifference, minimization, or avoidance runs low. The situation looks and feels so very black and white to the survivor. Those who are not allies and advocates for truth and justice are implicitly perceived as supporters of the murderer. Many survivors respond by retreating to a smaller, more trusted, and more predictable social circle.

Murder exploits the most basic of trusts and leaves us starving for a sense of safety and security. Connection with other human beings is one very important way that people normally seek security and safety. However, in the aftermath of murder, this option becomes challenged. Connection cannot exist without trust. Since our loved one was taken from us by the hand of another human being, many times by the hand of someone we knew or perhaps loved, it becomes harder to trust the next hand extended to us. Survivors of murder victims have seen the evil that can hide behind smiling faces. How do we know if the next extended hand is any different from the one that killed our loved one? How do we know what hands are safe to hold?

When we share our pains and fears, we are trusting others to validate us, comfort us, help us feel safe, or at the very least simply to *not* exploit the vulnerabilities we have revealed. This level of trust may seem like a reasonably attainable expectation, but in the aftermath of murder, it is actually a pretty hard order for any friend to fulfill and deliver flawlessly. Being a friend to a murder victim survivor can be an emotionally intense and burdensome endeavor even when it is carried out with love and good intention.

Not all friends will know how to help. Some may make us feel worse without even trying. It can be easy to mistake a friend's awkwardness and withdrawal as a sign of rejection or betrayal, when in reality, it may simply speak to the friend's inexperience and discomfort with grief. Not everyone has an innate sense of how to comfort and offer support to someone who is grieving. Learning to help others grieve is something that comes with experience, learning, and maturity. We learn to comfort and support the bereaved through the trials and errors of enduring other people's losses as well as our own. People who have experienced the death of a family member or close friend themselves often have more insight into the language of comforting the bereaved. Sometimes survivors are surprised by which friends are able to endure the emotional intensity of staying connected throughout the aftermath of murder and which friends disappear.

Secondary traumatization is real. Friends of survivors often feel profoundly affected by the murder. People can grieve the deaths of persons they never knew or people they only knew peripherally. Friends of survivors may struggle with their own emotional reactions even if they never knew the victim personally. Hearing of the murder, witnessing the anguish of the surviving family members firsthand, and watching the aftermath unfold are heartbreaking experiences. Some survivors are fortunate enough to have extraordinary friends who will walk through hell beside them. While it is not the friend's hell, it is hell nonetheless—a hell that they willfully visit to offer the survivor an anchor to the "normal" world, where the stuff of living continues to go on. Electing to visit this nightmare as it is played out in the survivor's real life is a test of courage and compassion—not a task for fair-weathered lightweights. It is not uncommon for survivors to go through a period of shedding friendships and shaking off loose social connections.

While the pain is very real to the friends of survivors, it is but a shadow compared to what the murder victim survivor is going through. Friends may feel guilty or self-conscious about expressing their own needs and pain. Their trauma may go unattended because of their own secondary survivors' guilt about living a life that has not been touched by such horror and loss. It is important for both survivors and their friends to know that being a loyal friend does not mean living the survivor's hell 24/7. The strength and value of the friendship may actually hinge upon the ability of the friend to keep one foot outside the survivor's hell and to willingly visit the trauma without fully internalizing it.

Murder has touched the survivor and come within half a step of where the survivor's friends are standing. The ripple left by murder can touch entire communities and even entire nations. The survivor's friends and community struggle to process and integrate the horror of the murder into the fabric of their lives too. Survivors, friends, and community members try to make sense of the incomprehensible. Everyone wants to know "why?"

The murder may bring friends of survivors to reflect on horror, loss, and grief from their own pasts and evoke the pain of past tragedies anew. While painful, these memories enable friends to relate more personally to what the survivor is experiencing. The ability and willingness of some people to transform their own pain into compassion for the survivor's situation can be phenomenal. Knowing that there are people out there who want to understand is healthy for survivors. It can be frustrating for friends to hear survivors saying how alone they feel in the world when everything inside the friend is screaming, "I'm with you. I am going through this with you. Although I may never know exactly what it is to experience what you are going through, I do know what it is to feel grief, loss, fear, horror, and rage. I can empathize with you. I am right here with you as close as I can be. Why can't you see me?" Friends need to understand that the loneliness of grief is not necessarily a reflection of the support or lack of support available to the survivor. Unfortunately, all the understanding in the world cannot relieve the loneliness of grief. Feelings of detachment and isolation are characteristic of both grief and posttrauma reactions. This loneliness is simply the aching for something that is no more. The best that friends can do is try to validate and comfort bouts of loneliness by simply listening and being there as a caring presence. Survivors often find it comforting to know that people are praying for their situation.

Some survivors will not have the emotional energy to look, listen, comprehend, or reflect upon what other people are going through even if it does relate to their own losses. Sometimes grief and trauma leave barely enough energy for us to make it through the day without falling apart. Emotionally intimate friendships take time and energy to maintain, some more than others. Survivors may regret that they just do not have enough emotional energy leftover to maintain high levels of supportiveness and closeness with a large circle of friends. The desire to be supportive and to forge mutual connections in their friendships has not died, but there is a shortage of fuel to propel that desire.

Some survivors get so immersed in their own pain that they develop this aura of owning the monopoly on pain and grief. Some survivors claim the monopoly for themselves by believing that because their loved one was murdered, their pain and grief are greater, or that their loss is somehow more significant because it evolved from murder. Those around them may feel as if the intensity of the survivor's grief invalidates or diminishes their own. Friends of survivors may find themselves qualifying their pain in conversations with the survivor. "...of course this is nothing compared to what you are going through." And when friends do not qualify their pain, survivors may catch themselves thinking those very words. Other times, people simply bestow this monopoly on grief and pain upon the survivor, whether or not the survivor wants it or the attention that comes with it. Either way, this monopoly on pain and grief inevitably evolves into isolation. Friends may stop seeking support from the murder victim survivor in relation to their own trials and tribulations for fear of adding to the survivor's emotional burdens. Yet, there are times when helping a friend with something that has nothing to do with murder could be absolutely refreshing to the survivor, like a reprieve from murder and a brief return to "normal life."

Many survivors isolate themselves from others by maintaining the belief that: "Nobody knows. Nobody will ever know. Nobody has ever known the grief, pain, and turmoil of what I am going through. Nobody else can understand. And in fact, this is so horrible, I don't want anyone else to fully understand. There is no point in bringing the rest of the world down with me." Many survivors become suffering heroes and simply stop seeking comfort and understanding from others. It is too painful for everyone. They retreat from human connection. Unfortunately, this scenario creates a self-fulfilling prophecy. If you stop communicating, you eliminate the possibility of finding the comfort and understanding that you most need to heal. Survivors do not heal in a vacuum; they heal through developing their sense of connection both in the spiritual world and in the world of people around us. We reclaim our desire to engage with the living by reaching for connection. If we refuse to reach, we risk getting stuck in a state of chronic existential loneliness.

Survivors may harbor fears of becoming high-maintenance friends to those around them. They may hold back from talking about the murder because they know their obsession with the murder has the potential to wear down the best of ears to sore little nubs. Some survivors panic socially when it dawns on them: "Oh my God, murder is all I talk about. Or all I want to talk about. Or all I can think about even when people are trying to talk to me about other things. I'm walking around with my head stuck in the grave and am out of touch with what is going on around me." The obsession with death and murder is a normal response to the loss and trauma. In fact, sometimes obsessive energy is downright necessary to fuel the charge for justice. Obsession can also serve as our psyche's high-powered, self-cleansing tool—a way of blasting the sludge of murder and evil from the interior of our minds, hearts, and souls.

Cleansing the poison of murder from our beings is a job that can only be done by the survivor, but it is also a job that should not be carried out completely alone. It is healthy for survivors to seek others to bear witness to the ugly legacy murder has left them to contend with. Sometimes survivors turn to friends, sometimes to strangers, sometimes to professionals, sometimes to other murder victim survivors, and sometimes to spirituality. Survivors can engage in support groups, on-line chat rooms and message boards created specifically for murder victim survivors, or they can simply seek people that are willing to listen compassionately to what they are going through. The more sources of support the survivor has, the less overwhelmed any one of their friends will be. If you do not have anyone to talk to about this, seek validation in publications like this one, write letters to imaginary friends, or talk to God or your higher power.

There will be friends who very quickly make the assumption that they have nothing to offer the murder victim survivor. You would be surprised at how many people cower and shy away from grieving hearts. They fear being swallowed whole if they come too close to the sucking chest wounds left behind by human mortality. Grief makes most people uncomfortable. When there is nothing that can be said or done to make anything better, it makes us all the more nervous about saying something wrong.

Sometimes the right words just do not seem to exist. The very phrases that offend some survivors bring other survivors comfort. Some survivors have no problem with the word "closure" because moving on as quickly as possible is their preferred coping mechanism. Other survivors might interpret the word "closure" to be a polite way of saying "get over it." At its best, people use the word "closure" with positive intents and wishes for healing. At its worst, people use the word to stifle the survivor's reaction to the murder to make themselves feel more comfortable.

Many people honestly do not know what to say to the bereaved so they grab words they heard someone else say and pass them on to the survivor without much thought—completely oblivious to the thoughts and feelings these words might trigger in the survivor. For the survivor who is already angry because they feel their loved one has been cheated out of a life they were meant to live, statements such as "it must have been their time to go" are simply out of sync with the survivor's reality. For the survivor who has not even begun to grieve, words such as "you're strong... I know you will find a way to put it behind you and get on with your life" may be interpreted as pressure to return to normal. When survivors are still being bombarded with images of their loved one's death and standing hip-deep in the pain and suffering their loved one endured, words such as "they're in a better place now" seem to shortchange the empathy and compassion the manner of their loved one's death deserves. Understating is like being given a Band-Aid instead of a purple heart. Yet there are other survivors who might utter these very words without pause to comfort themselves and others.

Friends often cannot navigate the fine line between triggering grief reactions by being too heavy and offending survivors by coming across as too trite, light, and insensitive to the gravity of their situation. Even validating the survivor's outrage over the murder gets tricky. It is disconcerting to the survivor to hear people say things such as "fry the murdering bastard" if that is not where the survivor is at in their own internal search for justice. Or, if the survivor emphatically wants to scream "hang the son of a bitch," it is hard to hear others express anything less than that.

Finding the right words can get very complicated. The survivor's reaction to the comforts and condolences of others can have as much to do with where the survivor is at in their grief, how they grieve, their values, and their definitions of justice, as it has to do with the actual words that were uttered. As a result, friends and survivors may just stop talking about the murder. Feelings of helplessness and powerlessness paralyze the friendship and an awkwardness pervades. Sometimes the awkwardness is due to both parties leaving it to the other party to bring up the unspeakable topic that hangs between them. Sometimes the awkwardness is due to a sense of failing each other. The survivor has failed to feel good for their friend, and their friend has failed to make them feel good again.

Survivors often feel an intense need to talk about the murder but may not be sure how to approach the topic with people. Communication about the murder is surrounded with social anxiety and an awkward emotional intensity. If we do not show enough emotion, it frightens people. And, if we show "too much" emotion it frightens people. Is it okay to talk about it? Is it okay not to talk about it? Will talking about the murder make the friendship harder or easier for the other person? Will it make it harder or easier for the survivor? Is it better for the survivor to tell their boss and coworkers what they are going through, or will it create complications with work relations? Survivors may hold back from talking about the murder for fear of being perceived as obsessed with it, while the survivor's friends and associates may hold back from talking about the murder to avoid being perceived as nosy or morbidly curious. Both parties need and want to talk, but instead, each remains silent to ease the pain of the other.

Survivors struggle regarding what aspects of the murder are appropriate for discussion, when, and with whom. Homicidal grief does not generally make good party discussion or office talk. We have to consider and negotiate the appropriateness of discussing the murder in all of our relationships and all of the social settings in which we exist and participate.

The belief that the murder is inappropriate to talk about can stem from the survivor's unresolved feelings of fear, guilt, and shame. "Will I make others feel uncomfortable?" "Will the horror of my loved one's murder traumatize my friends?" "Will information I share end up in the wrong hands and become grist in the rumor mill?" Survivors may want to talk about the murder, but fear of losing control of their emotions silences them. "Will I scare off my friends by talking about it too much or crying about it too much?" These considerations are part of surviving socially in the aftermath of murder.

Considering the nature of the information we share with

others and how it could potentially affect the murder case if it were to fall into the wrong hands is critical for survivors. Many survivors are forced to be silent by the need to protect the integrity of the facts and evidence at the very time they most need to talk. Even when survivors do venture to discuss the murder, it is not uncommon to sense some people shying away. The murder frightens them, and they want to get as far away from it as they can. They panic at the realization, "Oh my God, if it can happen to them it can happen to me." They do not want to see or experience the reality of murder vicariously through the survivor. It is too real and it is too close to home. Murder is only safe to them if it is on a television screen or in a book. Some people fear that if they learn too much about the murder from the survivor that they will end up being drawn into the horror. "Will the murderer come after me for what I know? Are the police going to question me because I associate with people directly involved? What if there is dirt in my own house that I fear being revealed if I am investigated or if my name should somehow make it into a reporter's hands?"

Survivors often feel alienated by the publicity of the murder case. Being in the public eye, stuck on the wide end of the telescope, can create an incredible sense of isolation, especially when we, or our loved one, gets lost and distorted in the public picture. If it is in the media, it is fair game for conversation—with or without the survivor's knowledge. Murder cases can become very political and economic points of interest in the community. The politics can be intimidating to survivors and friends of survivors. People often retreat from the glare of the public eye that surrounds murder. They see the rumor mill churning. They see the dump truck of homicidal grief approaching,. They see the "big eye" of the camera, and they run. People fear being drawn into something bigger than themselves. Survivors are frequently left to themselves to pick their way through the justice system and the media maze.

Sometimes it is simply awkward to know too much. Friends of the victim or friends of the survivor may find themselves unwillingly called upon to be ambassadors of information about the murder. Many people feel awkward asking surviving family members direct questions about the murder. They fear evoking an emotional response greater than what they can comfortably deal with, so they ask the survivor's friends instead. It seems no matter what is said or not said, rumors still abound and awkward questions of trust and confidentiality can emerge. Friends also may become privy to information that the survivor has not even heard. It is not uncommon for various renditions of the gory details of the murder to get passed along the grapevine. Friends of survivors may find themselves in the precarious position of choosing whether or not the survivor needs to know all that they have heard, and whether or not they are obligated to tell them. Sometimes more information, especially rumored information, only serves to upset, distract, and complicate. Yet, at other times it can bring important revelations to the case.

Even when survivors are successful in finding support and comfort in friends and family, they still may have to contend with a whole new set of adversaries in their lives—the murderer, any accomplices, the murderer's friends, the murderer's advocates, and perhaps the murderer's family. It can take some time to figure out who is adversarial to justice and who is an advocate of justice. Law enforcement, justice officials, and the media have the potential to be powerful allies or powerful adversaries in the aftermath of murder. Survivors often feel betrayed by the failures of those who by profession are expected to help re-establish some semblance of justice and public safety. Survivors are often rudely awakened by the realization that there really is very little protection to be had in our society to keep us safe from violence. Most people just believe in the illusion of safety and are much more vulnerable than they think. Survivors are often overwhelmed by the feeling of being on their own in terms of safety and justice and may feel driven to take steps towards being self-sufficient in their own personal protection. Sometimes these steps bring empowerment and connection, and sometimes they lead survivors to become lonely hyper-vigilant watchdogs that experience the world with a fence around themselves.

The ability to overcome the isolation and loneliness of homicidal grief ultimately depends upon re-establishing and maintaining relationships with the living as well as forging a new sense of connection with our deceased loved one. If we are not secure in our sense of connection with our deceased loved one, we may become frozen in time—afraid that living, changing, and healing will mean moving away from our loved one. Likewise, if we cannot re-establish our desire and ability to connect with those living, we also run the risk of becoming socially stagnant and left behind by the wagon train.

CHAPTER SIX

The Illusion of Fear and Safety

When the worst thing you can imagine happens, all horrible things become realistic possibilities. The illusion of safety is pierced. Every fear, every precaution becomes as legitimate as your loved one is dead. There is no such thing as paranoia in a world without safety. The boundaries that define legitimate fear, caution, and denial of danger become blurred. There is no comfortable gray area between reckless and hyper-vigilant. Even among family, friends, and professionals, it can be hard to figure out who to trust. Fear can be isolating. Fear carries a stigma of implied powerlessness and loss of control.

Prior to Sept. 11, 2001, I wrote the following: "It is hard for people to reach out their hand to fear because they just don't want to believe it is real. We live in a society that closes its eyes to the terror around them so they can believe fear only exists in movies, children's imaginations, mental illness, and seedy lifestyles. We buy into the notion that normal people, with normal lives, have little to fear. That dose of denial has been taken away from murder victim survivors." Later I wrote: "I wish with all my heart that I could still feel as isolated in my fear as the presumptive statement above suggests, but I know better now. I looked into the face of every person I passed on Sept. 11. In the faces of strangers, I saw a fear, horror, and anguish like I had seen only once before. In the faces of strangers, I saw the faces of all who mourned my brother's murder with me. Even now, months later, I still see glimpses of those faces—at work, at the grocery store, and at home. I know that America understands the fear I am talking about. I mourn America's loss of innocence." The naiveté of those untouched by violence is something to be cherished, not criticized.

The fears are many, and those fears manifest in a multitude of ways. Fear of the murderer is usually at the top of the list, especially if the murderer is free. Since friends and family are the ones who knew the victim best, they are often the first to hear the "warning bell" ringing. They are usually the first to know that something is very wrong and the first to detect any lies surrounding their loved one's death. They are the ones most likely to know who might want to harm their loved one. They are often the first to come forth with information that can spark or fuel a murder investigation and they are typically the ones who advocate hardest for justice. There are many murders that would not have been detected or solved if it were not for the persistence of the victim's friends and family. There are also many murderers who would have been released from prison years earlier had it not been for the efforts of the victim's survivors to block parole. Many murderers are released despite efforts to protect society from repeat offenders. Releasing convicted murderers puts survivors in a very targeted position.

Murder begets murder. Murderers will kill to cover up for lesser crimes and they will kill to cover up murder. Murderers do sometimes kill to retaliate against those they blame for their arrest and punishment. Fears of retaliation are not irrational. One person is already dead. How many murders does it take to know that there is legitimate reason to fear? Only one. And when 3,000 people are murdered at the hands of 19 in a matter of minutes, how do you handle that level of fear and unpredictability?

The fear that the murderer may someday do to other innocent unsuspecting people what they did to your loved one is always there. The more killers kill, the easier it becomes to kill again and again and again. Every unsolved and unprosecuted murder sends a message of empowerment to all murderers. The more killers get away with murder, the more murder becomes a viable means of getting what they want. The United States went to war in 2001 to teach the world that terrorism and murder are not acceptable means of getting needs met and it will not be tolerated. We need this same level of commitment to investigating and prosecuting the average 18,736 individual murders that occur every year in the United States (Maguire and Pastore, p. 308). According to federal statistics, almost one-third of all murders remain unsolved (U.S. Department of Justice, Bureau of Justice Statistics). In many cities and regions, the statistics are worse than that.

The fear becomes intensified when we do not see our law enforcement and criminal justice systems working effectively to send a clear message: "Murder won't be tolerated." Instead, we see far too many cases where evidence is not strong enough to result in an arrest. We see reduced charges, plea bargains, and acquittals. We see murderers walking free. We see retaliation against witnesses turning them into examples intended to intimidate entire communities into silence. Survivors see murderers swaggering with the perceived power that comes with "getting away with murder."

Even when a murderer serves time for killing, the fear that they might be released is always lurking. Incarceration is seldom a compassion-building experience. All murderers learn from their mistakes. Some learn not to kill. Others learn how to kill better. Very few murderers get sentences that assure they will spend the rest of their lives behind bars. There is the possibility of appeals, writs of habeas corpus, retrials, paroles, pardons, retroactive changes in the law, informant deals, escapes, administrative mistakes, and other loopholes which defense attorneys find to get a criminal released. The fear of retaliation among survivors and witnesses hovers imminently.

Fear becomes more complicated if we knew the murderer. Sometimes the murderer is a friend or family member—someone we had never thought of as a dangerous person. Sometimes it is someone we loved. If someone we thought we knew could do this, what other evil and danger are lurking out there behind the smiling faces of friends and strangers? Or, if we always "had a feeling" that someday, somehow this person would hurt someone, how do we deal with the fact that we and others were not able to stop the foreseen tragedy from happening? How do we react the next time we "have a feeling" that something bad is coming? What if we are the only one that takes our "feeling" seriously? We "had a feeling" before and look what happened. Someone is dead. The police do not protect us from our fears, and law enforcement generally kicks in after violence has occurred—not before. What if we get that same "feeling" in response to the stranger on the crowded elevator or to our neighbor down the street? Or when we are walking to our car? Or when we are home alone? Fears commonly dispelled by others as paranoia may actually be part of the survivor's experience-honed capacity to sense malevolent intent. Survivors comprehend the prevalence of violence and know the presence of evil. They have felt it at least once before.

Many murder victim survivors are disillusioned to find that conviction, imprisonment, and even execution of the murderer is not enough to restore their sense of safety in the world. The fear extends beyond the murderer. What about all the other murderers in the world? In the last ten years, the number of deaths ruled as murder in the United States has ranged from 12,658 to 23,271 per year (Maguire and Pastore, p. 308). Another thought to consider is that the murderers who are responsible for the years with our country's highest murder rates are now approaching parole eligibility. To a large extent, the safety of our communities from violent criminals hinges on parole board decisions taking place right now. Most community members are relatively uninformed regarding parole hearings and parolees released into their community. Organizations dealing with survivor support and victims' rights often monitor upcoming parole proceedings and notify interested groups and individuals in an effort to support parole block initiatives.

How many murderers do get away with murder and move on with even more confidence in killing? How many terrorist cells are still active inside our borders? How many accidents and suicides are really murders? If this can happen to someone we love, who else can it happen to? If this can happen to 3,000 people in 20 minutes, who else can it happen to? "Anyone" is the answer. When we begin to look at the number of murders (an average of 18,736 per year over the past ten years), the sentence served by murderers (the average time served by federal prisoners for murder is five years), the number of unsolved murders (approximately one-third), and the number of known murderers who were not successfully prosecuted, we begin to realize there are a lot of dangerous people in the free world (Maguire and Pastore, pp. 308 & 528). In a world like this, how do we come to trust anyone? How do we feel safe? The vulnerability and powerlessness leave us bare in a dangerous, unpredictable, and uncontrollable world.

Some murder victim survivors respond to fear by withdrawing from existing relationships or holding back from establishing new ones. They choose loneliness over risk of loss. If you do not get close, there will be less to miss when another is gone. When you do not know who to trust, the solution is to trust no one. Some murder victim survivors take this to the extreme and literally run away with their fears. They try to disappear, going through a period of drifting, homelessness, and hiding out to be sure they cannot be tracked down. Some develop plans to disappear if necessary, and others fantasize about it. Some move, change jobs, change names—anything—to stay one step ahead of the fear. The most frightening thing to realize is that it is not always fear driving them to these extremes, many times it is reality.

Some murder victim survivors handle their fear by sharpening their anger into spines that they wear like a porcupine. So much of the anger and rage that murder victim survivors experience are really fear of further loss and victimization. Murder turns up the fear, shortens the fuse, and sensitizes the trigger. We find ourselves being defensive where we once were open minded, accusatory where we once gave people the benefit of the doubt, and suspicious instead of merely interested. Anger is a normal defense mechanism for fear as noted by the fight or flight response. The best way to understand our fears is to understand our anger.

Some murder victim survivors take extra precautions to secure their homes and protect their families. They build fences, purchase alarm systems, guard dogs, and weapons—things that used to be unnecessary, perhaps even unthinkable. Many wrestle with how far they should go. Fear can block you from your ideals. People, who once were adamantly against guns, find themselves owning one. Some survivors even seek permits to carry concealed weapons. When does well-protected crossover into the realm of fanatical? It does not, as long as you are responsible and rational about your own self-defense—lock up weapons, keep them away from children, be well trained and well practiced, and be honest with yourself about your intentions and your ability to think and act rationally. There is no shame in doing what you have to do to feel safe and prepared, and there is no shame in deciding it is dangerous for you to own a gun in your particular emotional state and anxiety level. Precautions can and have saved lives, but they can also cost lives if not handled well. If nothing else, weapons of defense have helped many people sleep better at night. But remember, self-defense is not defined by your level of fear or anger alone; it is defined by the immediate threat. In the end, if you do hurt someone in defense of yourself, your family, or your home, even if it is the murderer, self-defense will be defined by people who are strangers to your situation, such as a jury, the media, or the police. Your fear and anger may even be used to discredit your reasoning. Your anger could be exploited as premeditated retaliation when you simply armed yourself in the event the murderer returned to retaliate.

Fear can drive people to violence as quick as anger. This is how violence spreads. We are all as susceptible to our fears as the common cold, and we are all more susceptible to violence than we would like to believe. The lines between fear and violence can get blurry, especially in extreme situations such as when a loved one has been murdered. Unabated fear can whittle logic into hysterics and make us very unpredictable in regards to how we respond to danger. Sometimes we flee. Sometimes we fight. Sometimes we freeze, submit, and wave the white flag to save our lives. Our response to fear can have a direct bearing on how we define ourselves—hero, coward, determined, victim, traitor, etc. Sometimes we do things in response to fear that we are not proud of. Sometimes we do the right thing no matter how scared we are.

Some murder victim survivors become so afraid of future losses that they smother their family and friends with worry. We try to control our fears by controlling others. "Please don't go on that trip." "Please don't move away to college." "Please don't work late." "I don't trust that boy you are dating." "No, you can't go out with your friends tonight." We become afraid that every parting could be the last. We think about everything that can happen when those we love are out of sight. Fear can be selfish, and we may want to hold back our loved ones to keep them safe even though we know it would be healthier for them to branch out and grow independently into the world around them. Fear is realizing you cannot protect your loved ones or yourself 24/7.

There are things we can do to counter the selfish side of fear. If you are living in fear that every encounter will be the last, go ahead and treat each moment as if it were the precious last. This is the healthiest thing we can do. Seek feedback. Ask those around you how your fears and protectiveness are affecting them. You must question yourself hard. "What special powers do I have that my loved ones do not? Why do I believe they will be safer in my presence than anywhere else?" The world is dangerous and there are no guarantees of safety anywhere. Period. Could it be that restricting them and holding them near does more to make you feel safe than it does to make them safer? Weigh quality of life against the measures you take to feel safe. What is the cost of that illusion you call safety, and what are you willing to pay?

Some survivors cope with their fear by inviting opportunities to defy it. They get reckless with survival like the soldier that just bolts from the foxhole into the open, not to escape the fear, but to face it and get it over with. When our heart has been ripped from our chest, we believe nothing can make us bleed. We may find ourself taking risks we never would have considered before— openly confronting people we might normally tolerate quietly, flaunting a disrespectful attitude toward authority, breaking the law, etc. Although this attitude and this energy can be very destructive, if harnessed by our values, conscience, and rational mind, the energy that is triggered by our fears and anger can carry us a long way through our healing. This is the same courageous energy that might enable us to begin or rekindle a relationship, return home, learn to have fun again, or find new reasons for living.

What do we have to lose? Why not answer this question by trying to pursue what is best for ourselves, our loved ones, and our communities. So long as we are alive, no matter what the circumstances, the correct answer to the question, "What do we have to lose?" will always be "everything." Why not make that everything something really worth living and dying for?

In a world that has no guarantees for safety anywhere at anytime, it is healthy to turn to the spiritual world to find the peace and safety that this world is so sorely lacking. The answers to our prayers for peace and safety are not always found in the world around us, but rather in the world inside of us. Instead of prayers for safety being answered with world peace, we are gifted with peace in our hearts and the capacity to embrace with gratitude the moments of peace and safety that abbreviate violence. Instead of being answered by freedom from danger, we are gifted with the courage, strength, and intuition needed to persevere.

If we allow fear to take over our lives, we become secondary victims instead of survivors. We may introject the lack of security we feel in our world into lack of security in ourselves. The less we trust ourselves, the more vulnerable we become. Evil is attracted to fear. Evil thrives on fear. Protecting ourselves from the disease of violence entails protecting and fortifying our souls as well as our homes and finding constructive ways of managing our fear.

CHAPTER SEVEN

The Battle of Peace and Rage

Survivors often wonder, "Will I ever know peace again?" Even in the best of times, peace does not come easily. Peace is grown and cultivated as we evolve through good faith efforts, acts of reconciliation, mutual understandings, tolerance, and acceptance of ground rules for how we behave and treat one another. We would like peace to be a common goal of humanity, but it is not. Our sense of peace can crumble to the ground in an instant with one evil act. On Sept. 11, 2001, the United States experienced as a country what it is like to have the most basic sense of peace and safety violated. When someone we love is murdered, the normal pathways to peace get washed out. The act of murder is non-reconcilable, non-negotiable, intolerable, and incomprehensible. Initially, all murder leaves for us to work with is torrents of horror, pain, fear, and anger. How can a sense of peace be molded from such intense negative feelings?

You do not have to be at peace with the murder or the murderer to experience peace and be a peaceful human being. You only have to make peace with your own rage and bring it under the care of your heart and soul. Although the first inclination may be to re-establish peace by snuffing out rage, you must let your rage exist. You need the power inherent in your anger. Find a way to co-exist with your rage without rage destroying you or you destroying it. You will not know peace until you face your rage and harness it.

Rage is anger with half the brain, five times the muscle, and only a thread of self-control. Rage is an instinctive response that erupts from the bowels of our deepest fears and angers. It is the force of desperation that takes over when we feel threatened, powerless, and deeply injured. When we have little to lose because we have just lost everything and all peaceful modes of protection have failed us, rage is the weapon we reach for. Rage existed long before reason and civility, and long before right and wrong. It is a vestigial emotion that dates back to the days when humans defended themselves from wild, pre-historic beasts and were very much aware that there were two types of beings in the world—predator and prey. When harnessed appropriately, rage can make the difference between victim and survivor. Rage is powerful and pervasive, but also very primitive. Rage is not sophisticated enough to connect its object with its cause. Like a frightened animal, rage bites without fully understanding the source or intent of the perceived threat. If we do not learn to control and care for our rage, it will isolate and control us, and it has the potential to contaminate and desecrate everything that makes us peaceful, compassionate, loving human beings.

When someone we love is murdered, it is like being robbed and raped by a demon that spreads the seeds of hell inside us. Every facet of remaining a peaceful and compassionate person is instantly tested and continues to be tested repeatedly for years to come. Anger and rage of a magnitude we have never previously experienced start sprouting up all over the place—in our dreams, fantasies, impulses, bodies, language, relationships, and attitudes. We did not ask for this anger and rage. It was imposed upon us. But like it or not, it is ours to deal with now. And so we do, every day, trying to figure out what to do with the rage before it turns our blood into battery acid.

What should we do with it? There is just *too damn much* to be angry about! The atrocities of murder violate the most deep and sacred of human rules—rules born of the Spirit, rules born of our human conscience and compassion, rules that we have always depended upon to engender peace and safety in our lives, rules that make us human beings instead of human beasts. Faith in the rules made our loved one vulnerable instead of safe. The one who broke the rules is alive, and the one that lived by them is dead. The rules did not work and they continue to leave us vulnerable to anyone who chooses to break them. It just is not fair that the murderer is allowed to exist, protected from the fury of humanity by the very rules they chose to pervert and violate when they took our loved one's life. The more deeply we believed in the rules, the deeper the betrayal, the deeper the rage.

We have been robbed of something most precious and irreplaceable—a human life. Our loved one has been victimized, violated, and brutalized in horrible ways. Our loved one's life, death, memory, reputation, and possessions have all been stigmatized by these horrible murderous acts and these horrible murderous people. As survivors, we try to erase the desecration. We try to make the world understand. We try to make the world care as we do, but sometimes people simply do not understand or do not want to understand. The stigma continues to bleed, marking us as warriors in a war that we did not wage. At times, it can feel like we are fighting everyone—the murderer, the police, the media, the prosecutors, the defense attorneys, our friends and family, our communities, ourselves, and God. We are even fighting with other countries over how to handle murderers and terrorists. The aftermath of murder involves a lot of fighting and advocating. Feelings can get very intense and it can be hard to maintain composure. The fighting is rage bait, and when rage takes the bait, it is hard to stop the momentum. Losing control publicly undermines our credibility, yet it is hard to maintain control.

Our efforts to defend and honor our loved one are often met by a criminal justice system that is deaf to the rights of the dead. At times, it may seem the only way to make our loved one's voice heard is to yell. The dead cannot dial the phone to call the investigator to ask, "Why haven't you picked up the guy that shot me to death yet?" The dead cannot stand before a jury to tell their truth. Their truth is told by a medical examiner who never knew them. Many of the laws and rules of the courtroom hush the dead to avoid emotionally biasing the jury. God forbid the jury should hear the voice of the dead too clearly. God forbid the victim's story sadden and frighten the hearts of the jurors. God forbid our society respond to murder like human beings instead of techno-legal-bureaucrats. But in that same courtroom, the murderer's voice continues on, unstifled and insensitive to how the words and the lies are demeaning the victim. The victim's survivors are cast to the sidelines to watch as the media and the justice system afford attention and rights to the murderer that they simply do not deserve while the rights of our loved one fade into the white noise of a justice system hard at work.

Even when we retreat to the sanctity of our private memories, we discover that our fondest moments with our loved one have been tainted by murder. Thoughts of our loved one lead us to thoughts of the murder, which lead us to thoughts of the murderer, which lead us right back down Rage Road. There are times when all paths seem to lead there whether we want them to or not. There is just too much to be angry about.

When the most sacred of rules have been violated, it can feel as if all the rules we have lived and judged ourselves by no longer exist or no longer matter. Rage at the pathetic scum that killed our loved one and rage at the betrayal of our faith in humanity tempts us to throw the rulebook away and fight the murdering beasts on their terms instead of ours. At some point we must make a choice. Do we reject our beliefs about peace and humanity and set our rage loose in the world? Or, do we morally and spiritually grapple with our rage? Can we accept that our values and beliefs do more to keep us peaceful than they do to keep us safe? Do not delegate these decisions to your rage.

Rage may be a good foot soldier, but it is a lousy leader. It will charge into the dark realm pursuing the murderer fearlessly and tirelessly. The further we follow them, the more likely we are to find ourselves lost in the same darkness that took our loved one's life. Do not be fooled. The murderers would love for us to believe that our war against violence begins and ends with them. Do not relegate this kind of power to a heartless killer. Our power to persevere in this struggle will come with realizing that the real war begins and ends in our world, not the murderer's world.

When we look at the body parts of thousands of people strewn and buried in the rubble of the World Trade Center, at the crushed skull of a baby, at the burnt remnants of a 29-year-old man who was set on fire in his sleep, or at the fear frozen on the blue swollen face of a 40-year-old mother who was strangled with the tie of her bathrobe, everything in us rejects the notion that these things could have been done by a fellow humane being. The cruelty and selfishness of murder extend beyond our comprehension into a dark inhumane world that revolves around greed, fear, and power—a world inhabited by human beasts instead of humane beings. Our inherent understanding of what it means to be human makes it impossible to include the murderer in our definitions. What would it say about humankind and us if we considered the murderer to be one of us? Why should we have to lower the bar of humanity to septic levels to let in someone that is repulsive and dangerous to everything we love and value? Even at the shallow end of culpability, the murderer more closely resembles a rotten apple that should be tossed from the barrel or a dangerous diseased dog that would normally be shot in the street, if it were not for the human face on its head. When the murderer ceases to be human to us, we are tempted to react in ways that are most certainly justified, but are less than humane.

We try to make sense of this dark world using the values of our heart and spirit, but find ourselves circling back again and again to the uncomfortable conclusion that the very qualities that make us peaceful, loving beings, such as our willingness to help, befriend, and find the good in one another also serve as the red carpet to these insidious, compassionless, murdering monsters. They wander into our lives disguised as human to rape, pillage, and strip us down until all that is left is bare rage and a thin cloak of faith that does not seem to keep us as warm as it used to. It is in this context that survivors find themselves weighing the fundamental value of life—our life, our loved one's life, the murderer's life, the lives of the innocent unsuspecting victims to come—all life. No matter how we try to price it, the value we place on the lives of others, even the life of murdering scum, is calculated into the price we place on our own life. Murderers certainly deserve to be treated with the same inhumanity they inflicted on our loved ones, but how do we achieve that consequence without devaluing our own lives or tainting our own spirits? Our concepts of earthly justice and fundamental spiritual beliefs lock horns.

We thirst to sic our rage on the murderer. But at what point would we decide the punishment was just? At what point would our rage be satiated? After the human beast has been shackled and caged? After the beast has been beaten? Tortured? Or put out of its miserable, value-less life? What if we spend a lifetime unleashing our rage and still find no justice, no satisfaction, and no peace. What would a lifetime of delivering our rage onto a worthless murdering piece of shit do to us? Even after we are gone, the murderer will still be a worthless murdering piece of scum. So the real question we need to consider is not "what does the murderer deserve?" it is "what do we deserve?"

Murder is so depraved that to inflict any aspect of it, even on the likes of the killer, entails crossing over that boundary of human-ness that distinguishes us from them. Which is worse, risking that yet another innocent life may die at the hands of a murderer or looking in the mirror every morning and seeing a murderer? When we are confronted with these choices, we should not allow our rage to have a deciding vote. Rage is incapable of making these emotional and spiritually-laden distinctions. It is important to hold ourselves to a higher standard of conduct than the perpetrators. If we do not, our quest for justice and peace will be perverted into a backyard brawl between two bullies who deserve each other as enemies. Our battle is more than that. The struggle is a test of our moral courage. How we wage the battle is about who and what we are.

We need to become keen observers of ourselves to recognize and deal with our rage. Rage sometimes seethes instead of erupts and it can look like many things. Are you feeling depressed and down trodden? Internalized rage frequently masquerades as depression and low self-esteem. Are you haunted by replays of your loved one's death and images of how you might avenge their murder? Are you suffering from stress-related health problems such as high blood pressure, headaches, and insomnia? Are you being cold and withdrawn? Distrusting and accusatory? Short-tempered? Resentful? Reacting to others with intensity out of proportion to the particular situation at hand? Is your threshold of tolerance low?

When you are pre-occupied within the private confines of your mind rehearsing the messages you want the murderer to hear, you need to be aware of what messages you are unwittingly sending to those around you who do not deserve your rage. Are you unable to hear the opinions of others, especially opinions about the murder, the murderer, law enforcement, or the justice system? Do you take the time to communicate about what you are experiencing or do you get impatient and just blast your pain into the faces of the ignorant so they might, for just one moment, understand what you are going through? Do you feel like it just does not matter who you piss off anymore? Do you feel that you have so much rage it is pointless to even process it all, or dangerous to even try? These are all examples of the ways rage can manifest.

Our reactions to our own rage and violent impulses can be confusing. On the one hand, our rage validates the depth and intensity of our loss and acknowledges our comprehension of the sacred rules that the murderer violated. Likewise, our losses justify the rage. What would it say about us, about our value of human life, and our feelings about the victim, if we were only annoyed about our loved one being violated and victimized? Naturally, we want the murderer to realize and feel the all the pain they created. Yet on the other hand, survivors might also feel ashamed and disgusted by their own violent thoughts and fantasies. In one moment we are reaping imaginary satisfaction from the imagery of our rage and violent impulses, and in the next moment we are horrified, asking ourselves, "Oh my God, what have I become?" We have become the survivors of murder victims.

Do not inflict the murderer's hatred onto yourself because of a rageful fantasy or feeling. Self-loathing is what the murderer deserves to feel—not you. Do not turn that sick uncomfortable revolting feeling in your belly upon yourself. It is merely a warning bell reminding you how you could feel if you were to act out your violent impulses and fantasies. That feeling is a sign that your conscience is still functioning. Rather than judge your impulses and fantasies, just identify them for what they are. If you picture yourself beating the crap out of the murderer until their bloody mouth pleads for their life, instead of saying to yourself, "What is wrong with me for thinking these things?" try saying "This is merely a picture of my rage, a normal reaction to murder." Although the feelings you may have in response to your own raging thoughts can be very disconcerting, the discomfort you feel is telling you something very fundamentally good about yourself.

Most murder victim survivors have thoughts, impulses, and fantasies about murdering, torturing, or hurting the perpetrator. This is the most frightening aspect of a survivor's rage. The normal anger of grief, compounded by anger about the murderous act itself, compounded by the frustrations and failures of justice, together fuel a rage capable of single-handedly carrying out "eye for an eye" justice. Even though the murder justifies your rage from here to eternity and back, it does not mean you have to make all of that rage yours. You are not obligated to carry all of that rage on your back or act it out.

The more shame you have about your rage, the more power rage will have over you. Embrace rage as an acceptable and under-standable reaction—a reaction that needs to be heard and har-nessed, not squelched. Recognize your violent thoughts, impulses, and fantasies of revenge as a healthy way of releasing your rage—a healthy way for you to play out your never-ending desire to protect and be a hero to your loved one—a way for your psyche to re-establish a balance of power between yourself and the perpe-trator. If you use your fantasy life to better understand your needs and feelings, these fantasies can aid in your healing. These fanta-sies are harmless if you do not act on them, and in the end, they might help you diffuse the desire to actually act out your rage against another. The violent thoughts and fantasies will fade when you do not need them anymore.

Violent thoughts and impulses can be confusing. They may lead us to inadvertently identify with the perpetrator. As we come to understand what circumstances make us want to kill, we come one step closer to understanding how circumstances could lead some-one else to kill. The leap from being an angry person with a cause to a murderer can be frighteningly small. But there are essential differ-ences between being a victim, a survivor, and a perpetrator. Most survivors have opportunities to act on their impulses of rage, but they choose not to. Survivors frequently have to endure the mur-derer in their presence at the funeral, before the investigation has culminated in arrest, while the murderer is out on bail, in the court-room, or after the murderer has been released.

Some survivors never have any reprieve. Their loved one's murder is never solved or successfully prosecuted. They have to endure the murderer's freedom day-in and day-out and somehow manage to maintain peace. I marvel at the strength and wisdom of these survivors and the faith they exercise in their own beliefs. How do they do it? The rage that must be stoked up daily at merely know-ing the murderer is free while their loved one is dead. The fears that must come up knowing that they, as well as so many other innocent unsuspecting individuals, are accessible to the murderers. The temptations that must come up, knowing that the murderers are accessible to them. If these survivors wanted to, they could measure up their own scoop of justice and give the murdering bastards what they deserve. Yet, all the survivors I know in this situation choose not to. In the face of their fear and rage, they still choose peace.

When we choose peace, we do it because we know we are stronger and wiser than the murderers will ever be. We know that we are sophisticated enough to see choices beyond predator and prey. We know that we are smart enough to see through evil's trick. We know that this is an opportunity to reject the horror that has touched our life by saying, "No more!" Take pride, satisfaction, and victory in knowing that unlike the murderer, whose only strength is in their willingness to use their forces of violence, we can control our rage and choose peace for ourselves. We are endowed with compassion and empathy that make it painful for us to act in ways that are less than humane. We need to remind ourselves that this is much more than a physical battle of differing forces. We are engaged in a full-fledged spiritual battle. If we can face our rage and still choose peace, we have won. The spiritual strength we have been reaching for is ours.

Only when we come to understand the depth of our rage and the magnitude of the spiritual battle that is being played out between our rage and our innate longing to simply know peace once again, only then can we really begin to dispel our rage. Internalized rage is a pressure cooker. If we do not recognize it and find ways to open the valves and release some of that pressure, we will eventually crack, spewing our rage over aspects of our lives that are too important to sabotage and disparage with anguish and violence.

The first step in harnessing our rage is recognizing it, targeting it appropriately, and finding ways of expressing it that do not hurt anybody and do not make us feel bad about ourselves. Initially, venting rage can feel a lot like drowning because we quickly find ourselves immersed in an outpouring that just keeps coming and coming and coming. Facing rage takes tremendous emotional courage, but the more we allow ourselves the time and freedom to vent, the more control we will have over how and when our rage comes out. By choosing to express our rage, we minimize the possibility of our rage popping up where it does not belong, such as in the courtroom, in front of the news camera, at work, or at the dinner table with our family.

Expressing rage is cathartic, a way of purging ourselves of feelings we do not want to act out. Expression is a way of derailing our violent impulses before they crash. We can actively express our rage through fantasy, art, words (both written and spoken), music, psycho-drama, target practice, physical exertion, throwing things, slamming things, smashing things, screaming and yelling. These things are okay so long as we are not hurting anyone, threatening anyone, or destroying property that is important to us or someone else. It is okay to put a dummy in a chair and pretend it is the murderer and do whatever we feel like doing and say whatever we feel like saying. It is okay to write unsent toxic pen letters to the murderer or to anyone else we are angry at. It is okay to make up horrible names for the murderer like scumbag, baby killer, slimeball, snake piss, rat turd, murdering puke, or simply coward. It is okay to scream until we cry and then scream some more.

If none of these options feel safe to you right now, it is okay to find a different starting point. There are more passive ways to catharsize your rage, such as bearing witness to someone else's rage. We may watch movies and read books with themes and struggles similar to the ones we are experiencing. Sometimes we need to see someone else express their rage to give us permission to express our own. Supportive interactions with other survivors can be invaluable in helping you find your rage and dispel it. Although there is a lot of rage work that you can do alone, it is safer and more effective if you have someone to do the work with, such as a close friend, other survivors, a counselor, member of the clergy, or someone else you trust. If you fantasize repeatedly about cutting off the limbs of the man that dismembered your daughter, tell someone. If you paint violent pictures that you keep hidden under your bed, show someone. The more your rage is seen and heard, the more the urge to act it out diminishes. Express your rage, express it, and express it more, until it strikes you as redundant instead of terrifying. The validation and comfort that others can lend to your expressions of rage will also help counter any shame you are experiencing. The presence of others to witness your rage adds a dimension of compassion to the process, helps give you courage, helps you maintain boundaries to keep the rage work safe, and even gives you a hand to hold as you discover all the other feelings that your rage was masking. Once the rage is cleared, our wounds and vulnerabilities may become more visible to us.

It is critical, however, that you do not attempt to undertake this kind of work with someone who cannot handle it or is likely to judge instead of understand. You do not need to be put in the position of caretaker when you need all your emotional resources to contend with the feelings that come up. And, the last thing you need is to have some one label you as "dangerous or scary" for trying to work through your feelings, or to have someone call the police because in a fit of rage, you said the wrong thing and expressed desires to do harm to the murderer.

Bearing witness to rage is not for the feint of heart. Even some counselors and clergy are not seasoned enough to deal with the rage that murder leaves behind. If the person you are confiding with makes you feel bad about yourself for feeling the way you do, it is a sign that this is not the right person to help you. Other murder victim survivors are usually the best equipped to understand and bear witness to your rage, especially if they have had some recovery time since the murder of their own loved one. They know first-hand what you are going through. Plus, helping you ultimately helps them as well.

If you are not ready to share your rage with anyone, or you feel that there is no one who can handle it or understand it, this does not mean you have to endure your rage alone. Try talking to yourself and to God. Let God see your rage. When you feel so full of your rage that you cannot stand it, turn to your higher power and say, "See. This is my rage. This is what I have to cope with every day. You need to know what this cruel senseless murder has done to me. You need to know how hard it is to remain peaceful when I see the dirty killer. You need to know that my heart is broken." If there is anyone in the universe capable of handling and understanding your rage, it is God. He knows what it is like to have a son murdered.

Along with seeking catharsis and validation for your rage,

you also need to gain a sense of control and mastery over it. Harsh self-judgment is not the same thing as self-control. If anything, lack of compassion for yourself can throw you out of control. If you judge yourself negatively for merely having rage, without patting yourself on the back for controlling it, it becomes a lose-lose situation no matter what you do. This scenario can ripen into a "screw it" attitude, which makes us more inclined to give into our violent impulses. Do not deny yourself the self-rewards of choosing peace just because you also feel rage. Peace is easy to choose when you are not angry. Choosing peace in the face of rage is a much greater spiritual victory.

Control over our rage comes from learning that rage can be expressed without someone being hurt. We learn this through expressing our rage and being there for others as they express theirs. This control also comes through paying attention to our rage and providing a structure within which it is allowed to exist. If we devote the time to express and work through our rage fully, our rage will come to trust that we will eventually deal with whatever comes up in all its intensity. This trust will better enable us to say, "No, not now. Not this way." to our rage when it does pop up in situations where it is not safe or appropriate to express it.

Another way of gaining control is to dis-empower the object of our rage. Dis-empower the murderers. See the murderers for what they are. The more scary we make them in our mind, the more rage they will evoke in us. Murderers are not powerful people; they are merely cowards who have no bottom line and live value-less lives. They are weak and spiritually starving because they are stupid enough to believe that violence can fulfill their needs and desires. Do not let the murderer de-value your life. Do not hand the reins of your emotions over to the murderer. When you think of the murderer, use imagery that truly fits their character—make them small, make them vile, and make them pathetic. With work and healing, eventually the murderer will seem not worthy of our energy or thoughts.

As out of place as it may seem, humor can be a very effective tool in managing rage. Although what happened to our loved one is not funny and wanting to bring the murderer in touch with the sick evil insanity of what they did is not funny, creating little imaginary scenarios with that perfect twist of mocking, humiliating, sarcastic humor can make the whole gear shaft of rage slip into something much healthier—a brief sense of satisfaction and a good belly laugh. Next time you notice yourself thinking about vengeance upon the murderer, try infusing your thoughts with humor. Instead of imagining yourself inflicting pain upon the murderer, imagine scenarios that make the murderer look stupid and laughable. Every good comedy is funnier if it is the bad guys who are fumbling and bumbling, taken aback, taken by surprise, shocked, and tricked. Combining rage with humor is healthy, not irreverent. It is appropriate, because humor dis-empowers the murderer in our mind and temporarily diffuses the emotional forces that drive rage to revenge. If we can laugh at something, it cannot have much power over us! If the belly laugh is big enough, then that grinding energy of rage gets spent in a way that ups our endorphin levels instead eroding our emotional fortitude.

Guided imagery, meditation, and visualization can be invaluable when coping with rage. There is a part of all of us that knows no words, and there are times in our healing journey when we must part from our words to move forward—times when we can verbalize the problems, the emotions, maybe even solutions, but still cannot seem to do a damn thing differently. "I keep snapping and yelling at the boys in my classroom, even though I know my anger is really at the three teenagers that beat my elderly mother to death for kicks. Even though I know this, I can't seem to stop yelling at all the teenage boys in my class." We cannot change until we learn something new, know it to the core of our being, assimilate it into our inner landscape, and let it be a part of us. We need to develop healthy self-talk and translate it into images, music, feelings, and symbols, before we can understand our messages on the core level. We have to talk to our rage.

Guided imagery can help us understand aspects of ourselves differently. If we do not like how we handle our anger and rage, we can envision our rage differently to teach ourselves, to the core, that rage can take many forms and we can control the form it takes. We can also use imagery to balance our rage. On the outside, murder leaves chaos. On the inside, rage, fear, and despair fight for space. The only way to anchor ourselves in this tornado of pain is to find something—anything—to balance the negativity. Imagery, meditation, and prayer are where we can find that balance. We can take our minds anywhere. We can sit still, close our eyes, go to new places, and before we know it, feel very different than we did five minutes ago. We say a prayer and feel the transformation that ensues. We can listen to music or a meditation tape and let someone else guide us. Or, we can just sit still until we can see and sense that part of ourselves that knows no words, and let it guide us. This is the part of us that holds secrets and keys that can open not just new ways of thinking, but also new ways of being and relating to the world. This is the part of ourselves we are talking to when we use imagery and meditation.

Expressing rage is hard, but letting go of rage can be even harder. Grief is exhausting. In the flatness of depression and despair, rage is one of the few things that can still make us feel alive. We need that rage to energize us so we can endure the long years that follow a murder. We need that rage to energize us in the fight for justice. We need that rage to fight on behalf of other victims and survivors. We may need that rage simply to ensure that we do not give up, that we do not give up getting up and functioning every day, that we do not give up caring, or that we do not give up fighting for what we believe in. We do not have to let go of rage. Rage is dogged, determined, and energizing, and we need that. Rage is a fire inside of us that we can let smolder, that we can stoke or pile with fuel, or that we can huddle around to get warm. Initially, this fire may hurt and burn inside us, but eventually, we learn how to control it and use it to further our healing and growth.

Grinding our rage between our teeth is an exhausting and painful way to start and end each day. There is no escape from the anger and rage, but if we search hard enough and long enough we might find that there can still be moments of peace inside of ourselves. The anger and rage will always be there to visit and stoke when we need to, just as our loved one will always be dead. The more we work with our rage, the more we learn that we can have moments of peace, and we can string those moments together into hours, then days, perhaps even weeks, if we are lucky. We do not have to become angry people to be true to ourselves and our loved one. We are still peaceful people, if we choose peace.

CHAPTER EIGHT

Justice and Revenge

Most of us have been spoonfed the fairy tale of justice in America since grade school. We believe in the system just because it is done the American way and we blindly assume that murderers will get "their due." Survivors of murder victims quickly learn that justice is not automatic. It is not guaranteed. Justice is something that has to be advocated for and fought for because we simply cannot depend upon others, even those paid and trained to enforce the law, to be as committed to the pursuit of justice for the victim as we are. We quickly learn that in the silent wilderness of ineptitude and bureaucratic inertia, the drive for justice easily slips back into neutral unless someone is constantly pushing it. All throughout our exhaustive fight for justice, most of us grapple with the question, "What exactly are we fighting for anyhow?"

What constitutes justice? In concept, justice involves maintaining and restoring fairness, truth, and honor to a situation. There is no way to restore fairness to a murder. We will never recoup our losses. No matter what happens to the murderer, he or she *did* get away with murder. Even if the murderer is locked up, tortured, and executed, our loved one is still dead. There is no justice for murder on earth. Justice is a myth, but our whole being screams for it anyhow.

The concept of justice gets rendered down to the practicality of extracting truth, determining guilt, delivering punishment, and protecting public safety. Although we can see pieces and fragments of justice here and there, the whole simply does not exist. Even the best-case scenarios of human justice are inherent with deep frustration for murder victim survivors. From there, it only gets worse when our criminal justice system answers our cravings for justice by serving up huge portions of techno-legal bureaucratic nonsense that in effect delay justice and focus more on protecting the rights of the criminal than the rights of the victim. In far too many instances, the system buries instead of resuscitates the pieces of justice that could be salvaged from the non-negotiable reality of murder.

Issues of guilt, innocence, and punishment are not decided on the truth. Justice is driven by a multitude of seemingly arbitrary factors, such as how well evidence is collected, the politics of the era and location where the murder occurred, how well the case was presented, and how convincing of a performance was done by a lawyer. The circumstances of the murder become bargaining chips in an intense negotiation of accountability. The excuses given for murder and the arguments for ignoring pieces of the truth are endless: "She was suffering from post-partum depression, therefore she should not be held guilty for drowning her five children." "The DA in this county is very conservative. She will not risk trying a murder case unless a body is found no matter how much evidence we have that her husband killed her and hid her body." "He was under the influence of crack cocaine when he killed her, therefore the charges will be reduced to manslaughter if he is willing to cooperate with police and hand over his supplier." "The murder scene was left unattended, therefore the evidence collected is considered contaminated and admissible in court." "Because the confession was made to his wife, she can rescind her statement to police that described details of the murder only the killer would know." Criminals do not get punished for the crime, they get punished for the evidence that actually makes it to the jury after being strained through that flimsy piece of cheesecloth we regard as the law.

By design, the guilty have the advantage in the battle for justice. Our system of justice fights vehemently for the rights of the criminal as well as the rights of the unjustly accused. "Innocent until proven guilty" builds our justice system on the premise that the accused have no responsibility to demonstrate or speak to their innocence. This is not surprising when we consider that our justice system was conceived in an era when people had just broke free of centuries of suffering at the hands of aristocratic abuse and tyranny. People were rightly more concerned about being victimized by the government than they were about being victimized by each other. Times have changed, the pendulum has swung full arc, and the system that once brought peace of mind to our citizens now leaves the front gate open to a nightmare. When someone we love is murdered, it becomes glaringly apparent how unbalanced the system is and how ineffective it is ensuring justice and protecting us from the predatory criminals that live among us.

Our system is riddled with opportunities for the guilty to wiggle free from the hold of accountability. The abundance of Boss Hogs, Barnie Fifes, and dirty cops in our law enforcement system ensure that many murderers remain invisible to justice. Key evidence gets overlooked or destroyed. Important leads get lost in stacks of phone messages. Witnesses and suspects are not asked the right questions. Inconsistencies in statements get missed. Even when the murderer is brought to face justice, prosecutors may be stripped of their most compelling arguments by exclusionary laws regarding admissibility of evidence.

If a defendant is tried for murder and found innocent, they can never be tried again for that murder no matter how conclusive the new evidence is. Yet, when the defendant is found guilty, appeals and retrials are usually sought and often granted. Even if convicted, our complex rules regarding sentencing, appeals, pardons, and parole give the murderer opportunities to attenuate their sentence. Our system does not offer any real sense of closure regarding how the murderer will be handled.

While the wheels of justice turn through these seemingly arbitrary and hairsplitting factors, survivors are left churning through every belief and value they once held. What should happen to the murderer? What do you do with murderers? What do you do with people that are willing to kill others for nominal personal gain? What do you do with people that do gruesome and horrific things to other people? What do you do with people that do things to other human beings that most of us would not even do to a cockroach? What do you do with people who treat human lives like pieces of toilet paper? How do you make sure they do not kill again? For the victim's survivors, what happens to the murderer becomes a very intense and personal issue that is interwoven with feelings of grief, fear, rage, anger, powerlessness, and betrayal.

Most survivors go through many stages of contemplating justice—what it is, what it should look like, and what it should feel like. Sometimes justice is knowing that the murderer will grow gray, lose their teeth, shrivel up, and die behind bars. For others, justice is watching the murderer hang, fry, breathe poisonous gas, or just get an injection, quiver and stop breathing. Some murders are so cruel and heinous that we cannot measure up a punishment equal to the crime without crossing that line that separates us from murderers. As we consider what the murderer deserves, we are forced to confront our beliefs about justice and peace. The boundary between justice and revenge and punishment and cruelty can be frighteningly thin.

As we ponder justice, we often find ourselves fantasizing about what should be done to the murderer. Most survivors want the murderer to feel every bit of the pain they inflicted on the victim and every bit of grief they inflicted on the survivors. We may want the murderer to feel what it is like to fear for their life. Perhaps this would make them think more about the value of the lives they have stolen. But then again, death is sometimes too kind. Perhaps they should suffer before divine justice delivers them to hell. Maybe pain could drive them to the empathy they lacked when they killed our loved ones. We may imagine ourselves inflicting the same tortuous deaths on the murderer as they imposed upon our loved ones. Perhaps a gun to the murderer's head would help them realize the magnitude of what they stole as their own life flashes before their eyes. Perhaps burning off just one limb would give my brother's murderer a taste of the fear and pain he inflicted on my brother when he doused him with accelerant and set him on fire.

The desire for the murderer to feel all the pain they created is not wrong. Wanting accountability does not make us vengeful, hate-filled people. Vengeful thoughts are a very normal part of surviving a murder, but it is important to recognize that our fantasies are fueled by more rage than reason and can easily cross over moral and ethical boundaries that were once an unquestionable given for us. If we allow our rage to paint the picture of justice for us and then enact the scene in real life, our once noble pursuit of justice gets perverted into actions that perpetuate violence rather than deliver justice. We end up with family feuds and gang wars instead of justice and healing.

While murder victim survivors have a high emotional stake in the outcome of the justice process, their influence over their loved one's case is very limited. The public, the media, the jury, the judge, the police, and the politicians all have more say in defining what justice will be. To the rest of the world, justice is accepted as whatever the jury, the judge, and the criminal justice system deliver. Sometimes what is delivered just is not good enough. When the outcome of the justice system is grossly misaligned with what the survivor's internal search for justice has found, it becomes a second loss, except this loss is at the very hands of those who are supposed to help and protect. This betrayal can burn like a hot coal in our gut and seriously taint our attitude toward law and authority.

The harder and longer a survivor has to fight for justice and the more public the fight becomes, the more likely members of the community are to misunderstand the survivor's aims. People start whispering things such as, "When are these people going to give it up?" "It's amazing the lengths some people will go for revenge." "They're taking this a little too far if you ask me." "If there was a case to be made, it would've been made by now." "I wish they would just get on with their lives ... I'm sick of hearing about it. "Survivors are often accused of being obsessed with revenge, when in actuality, they are committed to justice and the safety of others.

Every murder that goes unsolved, unprosecuted, or unpunished, is a slap in the face of justice and a threat to public safety. When a survivor fights to get a decent investigation, fights to keep their loved one's murder out of the cold case file, and refuses to let the murder and the victim be forgotten, they are serving as advocates for safety and justice, not advocates of revenge. Although the motives of survivors are personal, they serve the community as well. When encountering others that are too shortsighted to see this, be certain to dismiss their judgments. Do not allow them to engage you in arguments and dynamics that will distract you from your goals. Justice is also about preventing future murders.

Many survivors reach a point of defeated, heartbroken exasperation with the system when it begins to look like justice will never come. The temptation to bypass the system and exact justice independently can be compelling. It is much easier to resist the temptation to take justice into our own hands when we know the murderer is locked up and we and others are safe from further victimization at the murderer's hands. But, if the murderer walks free—ever— the survivor's urge to deliver justice personally is intensified by fear of retaliation, fear of re-victimization, and anger at the double injustice of a murderer living freely while their loved one is just as dead as the day they were murdered. Due to the large number of unsolved and unprosecuted murder cases and the number of paroles, pardons, and appeals that are given, very few murderers spend the rest of their lives in jail. Most survivors are confronted with the murderer's freedom at some point. Some have to cope with passing their loved one's murderer in the grocery store, seeing members of the community still accept the killer into their social circles, and watching the murderer live a life that our loved one will never have again.

Many survivors vow to find justice and protect others in their murdered loved one's name. However, there is a lot about justice that is simply beyond the survivor's control. Survivors need to be compassionate with themselves whether or not earthly justice is attained. Attainment of justice facilitates healing in many ways, but healing is not contingent upon justice. We must feel good about our efforts, and feel good about caring, regardless of the outcome. We must nourish our personal healing with the knowledge that we tried. It is futile to invest our wellness in the outcome of a system over which we have very little control. We owe it to ourselves to find a way to be okay and to experience happiness no matter what happens to the murderer.

Sometimes the only justice survivors find is in their beliefs regarding a higher universal system of justice that is flawless, a justice that is based on the truth—the whole truth, God's honest truth. This system ticks to the timeless clock of eternity that transforms lifetimes into seconds. God's justice is always at work, even when it seems imperceptible from where we are standing. We take it on faith that justice will be done, or not, and live with the consequences of our beliefs. When earthly justice fails, our faith in Divine justice may be the only road to peace we find. Our faith is one of the few things that cannot be taken from us, unless we give it away or abandon it.

CHAPTER NINE

Survivors' Guilt and Self-Esteem

The cascade of guilt that flows from murder is incredible. A child is murdered. The mother feels guilty. "I'm the one who gave my teenage son permission to stay out later the night he was killed." The father feels guilty. "Maybe if I had a closer relationship with my son, he would have told me about the dangerous situation he was in." The sister feels guilty. "I had a feeling something bad was going to happen. I knew the crowd my brother was starting to hang around with was no good, and I never said anything. I didn't want to get my brother in trouble, and now he is dead." The victim's best friend feels guilty. "He invited me to join him that night, and I said, 'No.' I wasn't there to protect him when he needed me most." The victim's most recent girlfriend feels guilty. "If I hadn't broke up with him, I think he would be alive today." Even complete strangers feel guilty. "I saw the gang hassling him about a half hour before they beat him to death. I wrote it off as boys' play. It didn't look that serious to me, and now that boy is dead. Maybe I should have intervened to break it up. Maybe I could have made a difference." The cascade of guilt just keeps pouring and pouring over everyone. Why is it, everyone feels soaked in guilt except the person who actually committed the murder?

Murderers and psychopaths tend to believe they are more powerful and intelligent because they can relinquish compassion and enjoy the false freedom of a remorseless existence. They revel in our guilt. They depend upon it. This is where they frequently look for their scapegoat, excuse, or justification for murder. Projected guilt is blame. Since the victim is no longer here to defend themselves and speak to their manner of death, the murderer often blames the victim. The murderer also may attempt to cast suspicion on any survivors who could serve as alternative suspects. If the murderer is arrested, a team of defense attorneys will join them in kicking up shame, blame, guilt, and failure everywhere—except where it belongs—to muddy the waters so the murderer can blend in better and evade detection. Although on the outside, murderers may look like the rest of us, they do not really blend in that well. On the inside, they do not grieve, they do not regret, and they are not horrified by the murder. You cannot really feel grief for the person you murdered if you cannot feel remorse for killing them. If you cannot feel grief, then you cannot know love. The murderer may feel immune to guilt, but this false immunity comes at a very high cost.

Internalized guilt is shame. Shame is when we start feeling bad about ourselves or those close to us on a level that goes much deeper than feeling guilty about mere actions and words. Shame is feeling bad about who you are. Guilt is feeling bad about what you do. In the aftermath of murder, shame, blame, guilt, and failure are major themes played out through the justice process. Unfortunately, law enforcement, the media, and the justice system have a way of making it feel like everyone is on trial—the murderer, the victim, the family, the friends, the spouse, etc. Defense attorneys are trained and paid to play on the guilt of victims, witnesses, survivors, and alternative suspects to raise doubts, erode confidence, and undermine credibility. You do not have to internalize all the guilt and responsibility that might be thrown your way throughout this ordeal. The more guilt you personally harbor, the harder it will be to defend yourself and your loved one from accusations and implications that are truly defense strategies and simply are not yours to carry. The challenge of deflecting guilt and shame that are not yours to bear can be intensified if your loved one's case is receiving a lot of media attention, if you are called upon to testify at the trial, or if the murderer has many friends and supporters in the community. Sometimes these people would rather blame the victims and survivors than face the fact that their friend or family member is a murderer.

If you are struggling with guilt, take a moment and pat yourself on the back. These feelings are telling you something fundamentally good about yourself. Your conscience is working. There is a lot to be learned by facing your guilt. Sometimes we learn how to be better people. Sometimes we learn how to be more compassionate with ourselves and others. Sometimes we learn how to free ourselves, or just learn to set the burden of guilt down for awhile. Sometimes we learn we are carrying guilt that is not ours. Sometimes we discover that we are not the only ones carrying the burden of our guilt. We are capable of blaming others in all the subtle and not so subtle ways that we blame ourselves. We may even feel guilty because we secretly harbor blame towards the victim or others. We may wonder what blame is being harbored against us as well. The aftermath of murder is layered with tremendous feelings of failure, guilt, blame, and shame. It can get difficult to distinguish whose is whose.

Although feelings of guilt and failure are a normal response to trauma and loss, chronically carrying and doling out responsibility for the murderous acts of someone else is not a healthy or constructive coping mechanism. You need the energy that guilt consumes to heal, to advocate for justice, and to fulfill your own life missions. Unresolved feelings of failure and guilt can quickly transform into shame, whittle away at your self-esteem, interfere negatively in your relationships, impact performance, isolate you from others, exacerbate depression and despair, and potentially damage every aspect of your life. Guilt is sneaky. It masquerades as many things such as depression, helplessness, control issues, an inflated sense of responsibility, perfectionism, resentment, enabling, or martyrdom. Sometimes guilt can motivate us to grow, but guilt can also gridlock us into emotional holding patterns that are very painful and hurtful. We may not realize that we are actually the ones gnawing on our own hindquarters, perpetuating our pain.

Surviving any death is humbling. Death brings us to our knees no matter where we are standing and leaves us shocked, stunned, and disoriented. We feel blinded and confused, shaking our heads "no" in deep pleas of disbelief. "If they no longer exist, how will I?" Grief cripples us to the core and brings into question everything about the meaning of life and our worth as human beings. Somehow, everything that comprises our lives and who we are no longer feels wholly our own anymore. The best of everything we are can be taken away in an instant. Does this make us worth more or less? Grief is not a bold parade of confidence back to normal life. It is a slow, solemn, and humble journey. Grief raises questions and doubts about ourselves, about others, about the world, about our higher belief systems, about the spiritual realm, and about good and evil. Grief is a time of intense contemplation through which we weigh the pain of all that life takes with it when it leaves against all the things about life that make it worth holding onto. We either come to terms with our powerlessness and vulnerability or we do not.

The pure horror and trauma of murder add sour grist to the grief mill tainting these deep and sacred contemplations. At our most humble and vulnerable moment, murder high-jacks our lives to dark places far from the lives we once knew, places dark with the worst of everything—death, violence, lies, cruelty, destruction, failures of human kind, failures of justice, and even failures of ourselves. Everything is wrong with the world, and there is not a thing we can do to change it. In this dark, dark environment, it gets hard to see ourselves or others very clearly. Feeling good about anything, even yourself, can be a huge challenge. Sometimes we stray so far in this dark, lonely land that we lose sight of the goals that once guided us and the accomplishments that once bolstered us through each day. Self-esteem gets lost somewhere amid the thick under-growth of horror and powerlessness leaving us vulnerable to un-founded feelings of guilt and responsibility. We may feel guilty for merely being alive or guilty for enjoying life without our loved one. We may curse ourselves because we cannot seem to stop the compounded losses that come with our prolonged struggle with grief and murder.

The impact of having a loved one murdered can be incapaci-tating. It is not unusual for survivors to lose friends, lose jobs, lose homes, lose family bonds, lose optimism, lose self-esteem, lose health, and lose faith in the aftermath of murder. Survivors commonly feel they are letting everyone down by not bouncing back quickly enough. Things that were once a routine part of everyday life be-come difficult to perform with any rhythm or vigor. We may find it hard to eat, sleep, concentrate, work, socialize, or carry on with fam-ily life. We worry that others will notice we are faltering. "I'm not finishing my work. I can't concentrate. My desk is piling higher and higher, but I just can't seem to bring any task to completion anymore. My boss is starting to resent picking up my slack. Why can't I just move on? How can I answer to them what I can't even answer to myself?" We may find it hard to accept that the murder has injured and victimized us too. We struggle in vain to win a battle that is over. We lost. The only way to move past this sense of failure and on to win the real war is to recognize our losses as mere facts, not personal failures. Not personalizing the vile acts of others as weaknesses or shortcomings in ourselves is not nearly as easy as it sounds.

Guilt and inadequacy confront survivors at every turn. We may feel ashamed of our own grief and anger; breaking down at times when we expect to be composed; lashing out and being defensive with others, even those who are just as injured as we are; not having the energy to smile and laugh when those around us are starving for fun and joy; or not being able to focus on the people and the day to day activities that scream for our attention. Grief has incredibly thin skin. Our threshold of tolerance is low. Everything feels like the last straw. Even fun things start feeling just like more pressure. Losing control over one's emotional landscape is a lot like trying to stop an avalanche. We feel inadequate to stop the rockslide of emotions that are burying every aspect of our life.

We may have a sense of failure for not knowing how to guide our friends and family members beyond the aftermath of murder. "How can I help them when I can't even help myself? My children who are still alive have lost a part of me as well as their sibling. I know my pain scares them, but I can't stop crying. I think they are holding back their grief to be strong for me, and that is so sad. I am the parent. I'm supposed to be strong for them." We become frustrated with ourselves for feeling too empty, tired, and injured to fill the void that has been left in our core. At the same time, we may feel guilty when we do find ways to carry on. We may believe that by engaging in life we are disengaging from our deceased loved ones. We are abandoning them, or giving away a part of ourselves that used to be for them. Harboring this kind of guilt brings the grieving process to a stalemate. We feel too guilty to allow ourselves to heal and then beat up ourselves for not healing fast enough.

Survivors sometimes feel ashamed of their behavior after the murder. We may feel ashamed for not seeking vengeance upon the murderer when we still had the opportunity. We may feel like we let the murderer get off easy by not making them answer directly to us about what they did. We may feel like we let our loved one down by not being with them when they died or viewing them after. Other survivors feel ashamed of their preoccupation with grief, justice, and revenge. Some feel guilty for not coping well with the murder, not being able to function, or not being able to break out of their mourning. Others feel guilty for not mourning enough. We may feel guilty about our regressions and relapses into dysfunction in the wake of murder, or we may just drive ourselves deeper into denial. Seemingly, all our coping mechanisms, healthy or not, kick-in with full force when we are in thrust into crisis.

Crisis often brings out the strength, courage, wisdom, and compassion in us. Sometimes death shocks the living into handling their life with more reverence and respect. People realize they better get on it before the clock runs out. Crisis and tragedy bring out the best and the worst in us. The ability to acknowledge both can help us make it through the aftermath of murder with our esteem and self-worth intact. Sometimes we focus only on the negative because we feel guilty for any positives we might derive from the murder. It can be hard to admit to growth and fulfillment that are derived directly or indirectly from someone else's death. This book is a good example. Completing a book and getting it published has been a lifelong dream of mine. My brother's death handed me a theme, brought me closely in touch with the material, and inspired me to follow through to completion. Is it disrespectful to couple our dreams and tragedies like this? No. Obviously I wish my brother could be alive to encourage me, but he is not, so I accept with tremendous gratitude whatever gifts of inspiration he can still give me from his grave. Just as I would never reject the gifts he gave me throughout his life, I would never reject the gifts and blessings that have evolved from him after his death.

Survivors may feel a tremendous amount of guilt and failure relating directly to the murder and the events that led to it, especially if the survivor witnessed the murder or was aware that their loved one was at risk. We were not able to help our loved one in their greatest hour of need. Survivors may picture themselves stopping bullets, running into burning buildings, and restraining raging homicidal beasts. We sometimes get our wishes and expectations confused in regards to what we should have or could have done. Survivors "could'a, should'a, would'a" themselves to death with scenarios that might have ended differently. "If only I hadn't cancelled my plans to visit my sister that night, she would be alive." "If only I had been physically stronger, I could have stopped him from beating my mother to death." "If only I had driven my son to school that day." "If only I had convinced my sister to leave her abusive husband." "If only we had taken the threat seriously."

We were not the ones presented with the choice to kill our loved one or let them live. The murderer made that choice and the guilt and the responsibility starts and ends right there. Stop your guilt lashings and repeat this message, "The murderer made the choice to kill. The guilt and the responsibility start and end right there." Do not prosecute yourself or anyone else but the murderer for your loved one's death. The murderer needs to be tried, not the survivors or the victims. Many horrible things happen that we cannot stop. Feeling falsely responsible evokes a false sense of control over life and death but changes nothing. You need to take the situation apart and analyze every component. Think realistically about the options you were presented, the confirmed information you had available to you, and the choices you made. More often than not, the unfolding of events did not even present us with the option to save our loved ones, but we feel like we should have saved them anyhow. We need to recognize the boundaries to our power and understand where our responsibility ends and some-one else's begins.

The stigma that murder places upon victims and survivors can reinforce feelings of guilt and failure. The public eye is on us under the worst of circumstances. We see our loved ones lives and deaths presented naked and raw before this elusive public eye that is not necessarily compassionate, knowledgeable, or even accountable. Public information and rumor are more impulsive and incomplete than they are accurate or comprehensive, but they sell newspapers and get ratings. Society wants an explanation for the murder just as we do. Members of the public hunger for reasons to let go of their anxiety and conclude that something like this could never happen to them. They naturally want to understand how things like this happen and learn something from someone else's misfortune so they can avoid such a fate themselves. I believe this sort of analysis of tragedy is a normal and adaptive societal reaction to violent and traumatic deaths. Unfortunately, the analysis sometimes renders judgment instead of wisdom. The victim and often the survivors are deemed "people who put themselves at risk with dangerous associations and lifestyles" by others who desperately want to believe that murder cannot touch their family.

Common human vulnerabilities and shortcomings, such as poor self-esteem, poor judgment, poor choice of friends, drug and alcohol use, mental illness, poverty and homelessness, hidden lies, infidelity, being in the wrong place at the wrong time, risky behaviors, hero complexes, lapses in parental supervision, or any myriad of personal frailties and indiscretions can be turned into defense strategies for the murderer, fodder for the media, and points of gossip throughout the community. If others can identify aspects of the victim's lifestyle that were "inferior" in some way to their own or that placed the victim at risk, then they have found grounds for feeling safe and in control of their lives again. "These things don't happen in my life because I don't let my children stay out after 9 pm." "My husband doesn't abuse me." "We don't associate with riffraff." "We don't live in a bad neighborhood." "We don't have drugs or alcohol in our house." "We don't own a gun." Survivors often feel alienated in their own communities, as if murder is contagious and they have been quarantined.

Although people don't mind reading about the murder in the papers and discussing it throughout the community, many are reluctant to hear the details from the perspective of those most affected, as if knowing too much might pierce their bubble of immunity from victimization. When survivors are vocal in their attempts to defend their loved one's reputation, members of the community often view the defensive behavior as a telltale sign that there is something to hide or something that needs explaining and qualifying. At the other extreme, survivors might be involuntarily called upon to engage in discussions about the murder that touch on highly personal matters that heighten feelings of vulnerability and shame. Survivors often must endure substantial questioning at the hands of investigators, the media, prosecutors, attorneys, and members of the community. The whole experience of being under the "big eye" may be new to the survivor, and they may feel bad about themselves for the public image they presented. The aftermath of murder is not a photogenic experience, but it does not stop the media from putting a camera in our face. Murder is not a situation that evokes our best public presence or speaking skills. Looking like a basket case, being in shock, rambling nervously on and on, acting like a fanatic bent on revenge, or appearing too composed for circumstances are all normal and acceptable reactions to having a loved one murdered. There is nothing to be ashamed of even if you do not like how you appeared on television or are not happy with the words the reporter chose to quote in the paper. It is essential to maintain some self compassion for what you were going through at the time and understand that handling the media, investigators, attorneys, etc., is a skill that evolves with experience. You will get better.

Some survivors place themselves in emotional double jeopardy by both internalizing the natural feelings of powerlessness that death brings and viewing their positions of powerlessness to be stigmas of failure. Death is non-negotiable. It leaves us painfully and acutely aware that we do not have control over the most critical life events. The victimization of murder intensifies these feelings of powerlessness. We not only feel powerless before God, powerless before nature, and powerless before mortality, but now we also feel powerless before the evil will of fellow human beings. We stand surrounded by a tender aura of vulnerability. We cannot undo or compensate for the atrocities that were committed, although our hero hearts long to turn back time and rescue our loved ones from their demise. There is not a damn thing we can do to ease anyone's pain or restore their losses. There is no way we can guarantee that something horrible like this will not happen again.

The workings of the justice system contribute to our feelings of powerlessness. It is natural to feel like it is our duty—our mission—to lead the call for justice. Yet in actuality, our system of law and justice has no place for us. We stand silently watching the passionless parade of justice. Our criminal justice system strives to cut the passion for justice out of the equation to keep it an objective process. Survivors are relegated to a most ambiguous and innocuous role in the investigation and prosecution of the murder. We are not the ones making the decisions about how to investigate and prosecute. We are not the ones interviewing the witnesses or asking the questions. We are not on the jury, we do not have a vote, and we do not have control over what the jurors hear and do not hear. We are instantly immersed into a system that we do not fully understand, a system clearly slanted against the vested interests of the victims, survivors, and public safety in general. There is very little we have control over in the process of justice. The extreme objectivity of the whole process can make us feel inappropriate for feeling passionate about justice. Victims and survivors are often as much on trial as the murderer. Defense tries to cast enough doubt to evade conviction. Do not internalize the strategies and processes of justice.

Survivors may feel frustrated and ineffectual in their desire to protect those they love. We may feel frustrated and ineffectual in the pursuit of justice on behalf of our loved one. We may fail to see that it is the system that is dysfunctional, not us, and not the victim. The murder is wrong, not the victim or the survivor. We may judge our feelings of powerlessness harshly instead of accepting that we are simply every bit as vulnerable as we feel.

Feelings of powerlessness often masquerade as feelings of guilt, failure, and responsibility. Trying to shoulder the responsibility emotionally is an attempt by the survivor to try to gain a piece of control in a world where we sometimes have no control or ability to stop horrible things from happening. We subscribe to the subconscious belief that if the problem is us, then the power to fix the problem lies in us. Letting go of our guilt and sense of responsibility means letting go of our hope that we can change the reality of murder, which ultimately entails facing our grief on deeper levels. Survivors may try to compensate for their feelings of powerlessness by wrapping their self-definitions of success and survival around efforts to regain control.

We may squelch our emotions to demonstrate our control over ourselves and our situation. We may try to compensate for the failures of the criminal justice system. We may become obsessed with the case, try to crack it, and try to find that one last piece of evidence that will assure a conviction. We may fantasize about hero-hood, about saving our loved one from their fate and teaching the murderer a thing or two. We may even bargain with God. "I will give you my life, if you deliver my daughter back to the people who love and miss her so deeply." We may find ourselves trying to regain control by controlling others, controlling our environment, and making rules both spoken and not. Or, we may find ourselves being more contemptuous of authority and quick to rebel both as a means of flexing our autonomy, but also as a means of expressing the disgust and disillusionment bred by the failures of the criminal justice system. We may sometimes wonder, "My God, who is this demanding controlling person I have become?" You have become a person struggling with their vulnerability, struggling to feel safe and in control in the wake of being violated by the most brutal violence known by humankind.

We may believe that had we been perfect, had the victim been perfect, or had others been perfect, the murder never would have happened. In the aftermath of murder, we may buy into the belief that if we can be perfect, we can compensate for everything that is not okay in our world. We can stop things like murder from happening again. If we are the perfect parent, the perfect child, the perfect employee, the perfect student, and/or the perfect friend, then the pain and loss of the murder will be diminished. This belief may even extend to those around us. We may start demanding perfection of our children, our friends, our spouses, our parents, our siblings, and our co-workers. Our reactions to normal mistakes, shortcomings, and vulnerabilities can become exaggerated and we may find ourselves repeatedly dumping the emotional weight of the murder on ourselves and those around us every time something goes wrong. The desire to fix and compensate for events that cannot be undone transforms into a "tear it down if it ain't perfect" attitude, and we turn everything that is wrong in the world against ourselves and others.

These irrational beliefs about perfection and control are very primitive developmentally and are just *soaked* in vanity and pride. We assume that the actions and consequences of the world revolve around us. We assume that perfection is attainable. People naturally go through developmental phases in childhood when they perceive themselves as the center of the world and the cause and solution to everything, which is why this kind of guilt reaction is so common among children in reaction to trauma and loss. Adults, however, are not immune. When overwhelmed with pain, we are at risk for regressing to this developmental level and adopting this reaction. Or, perhaps due to our own personal histories, we may have never developed beyond these irrational beliefs and coping mechanisms. Ultimately, perfection is a self-destructive, shallow, and boring goal that perpetuates our feelings of guilt and failure more than it relieves them. Expecting perfection ultimately erodes our esteem instead of building it because the belief that we could ever be perfect is nothing more than a self deception that precludes further growth. Overcoming guilt entails letting go of this false sense of control and pride. We overcome guilt, not by being perfect, but by being humble and embracing our vulnerabilities and the vulnerabilities of others as well.

Although it is critical to recognize the fundamental vulnerability we all share and to differentiate between the aspects of our situation that we can control and those we cannot, we also need to be careful not to confuse powerlessness and helplessness. Sometimes we may be quick to adopt a position of helplessness to avoid facing the real core of our guilt. For example, a child retreats to her closet to muffle the sound of her parents fighting in the other room. She starts to hear sounds of things being thrown and crashed. She hears her mother screaming to God for help. She wants to run out and help her mom, but she is frozen with fear. She cannot move. Eventually she hears silence and then her father's pacing footsteps. This little girl grows up believing she failed to save her mother. She misinterprets her survival instincts as cowardice. Her father goes to prison. She believes that had she been braver, she could have stopped him and saved him too. Socially, she finds she cannot stand up for herself and confront people. She is afraid of her courage. When she does express courage, she is overwhelmed with guilt. To embrace her courage, she has to face the self-implication that she had the resources to prevent her mother's murder, but for some reason did not use them. Subconsciously, to avoid facing her guilt, she avoids having courage. In this scenario, our successes and resourcefulness evoke guilt instead of bolstering esteem.

Learned helplessness is a self-defeating trap that brings our healing and growth to halt.

Powerless does not mean we are helpless. No matter what our situation, nothing can stop us from learning more about the challenges we face, nothing can stop us from defining our cause, nothing can stop us from advocating for ourselves by speaking our mind, and nothing can stop us from praying. We can be the voice of honor, outrage, and accountability on our loved one's behalf, and we can do this as loudly as we need to. We can take pride and support one another in our constructive and proactive efforts to hold violent criminals accountable for their actions. We can join the armies of citizens that fight the premature release of murderers from prison through demonstrations and letter writing campaigns. We can ask for maximum sentencing. We can let professionals within the system know that we care and are watching. We can redirect the energy currently being consumed by our guilt into proactive and empowering strategies.

Survivors often lose trust in their own judgment about what is safe and what is not. The world we trusted to be safe proved to be fatally cruel and dangerous. People and places we thought were safe were not. Our loss of self-trust further whittles at our confidence and self-esteem. Many survivors retreat in the aftermath of murder. They withdraw socially and stay closer to home. We might find it hard to muster the confidence and courage to do things that used to come naturally such as meeting people, socializing, staying out after dark, or being home alone. We might feel like we have regressed to cowardice and are retreating to a smaller world that is easier to control and manage.

Sometimes we feel inadequate because we just cannot make sense out of everything we are thinking and feeling in response to the murder. There are so many critical questions starting with "Why? Why? Why?" Those who pride themselves on their skills of analysis may perceive their inability to answer the existential questions that murder brings as an intellectual failure. "If only I could figure it out and find the key, I would be okay." Those who pride themselves on their faith may perceive their inability to satisfactorily explain the murder with their higher belief system as a spiritual failure. "If only I could get my faith back, I would be okay."

The murderer takes first and God answers questions later, perhaps not even in this lifetime.

The moral, cognitive, and spiritual dissonance buzzes inside our heads like old buck flies in a farmhouse window. The struggle is distracting as hell. The chronic confusion left behind by the murder interferes with our ability to make decisions in other arenas of our lives. We feel that we are owed an explanation and that life should not continue forward without one. The inability to comprehend the horror that was inflicted on our loved one makes everything about our loved one's death seem objectionable and unacceptable. Sometimes our objecting and rejecting attitudes spill over into the rest of our lives as well.

We may believe that we do not deserve to be alive any more than our loved ones deserve to be dead. Sometimes we feel guilty for merely being alive and enjoying life. Does it devalue our loved ones if we find a way to enjoy life just as much without them? Does it devalue our loved ones if their deaths free or inspire us to open doors that we never would have explored? "Is it okay to fall in love again, if the love of my life is dead?" "Is it okay to try to fill the void that has been left in my life?" When you experience twinges of guilt for living too fully while your loved one lies dead, remind yourself that the best you can do is honor them with your life. A wasted life is no honor. Their death was a reminder that life is precious and short. This is one aspect of your loved one's death that the shadow of murder can never touch. To live life and regard life as anything less than unique and precious, would be missing the very essence of your loved one's life and death.

We may wonder if we gave enough of ourselves to our loved one while they were here. "Was I a good enough parent?" "Was I a good enough sister?" "Was I a good enough friend?" What do we do if our gifts do not outweigh our trespasses and betrayals? Our level of guilt can be intensified by the issues that were playing out in our relationship with our loved one prior to the murder. We may feel plagued by these issues in our grief. It is too late to change or make restitution for anything. All we have left are unresolved issues and conflicts, things we wanted to do with and for our loved one, or things we wanted to say—and all of it is simply too late.

Some survivors never resolve leftover relationship issues with their deceased loved one. They live with the guilt, get very good at denial, or discover that death has a way of transforming many of our faults, conflicts, and issues into mere trivia. In the larger scale of life and death, it is irrelevant who stepped on whose toes. Ironically, we may even discover that the very things that annoyed us the most while our loved one was alive, are the very things we miss the most now that they are gone. For all we know, our loved one may be looking at our transgressions with the same level of forgiveness and understanding. Understanding what is really important and what is forgivable can go a long way toward relieving leftover guilt.

Sometimes letting go of guilt is not quite that easy, especially if it pertains to deeper issues. It is not uncommon for survivors to develop an idealized view of their relationship with their deceased loved one as a subconscious attempt to avoid confronting their underlying feelings of guilt and blame. Some idealizing is normal and healthy, but if our revisionist view of history strays too far from reality, we are in danger of evoking resentment from our loved ones who are still alive. Other siblings may resent following the footsteps of a sibling who is bigger than "real." Friends and family may become upset if we proclaim ourselves the "expert" on our deceased loved one, especially if our perspectives differ drastically from theirs.

Although your loved one is no longer here, you can still work through relationship issues with them. Guilt often manifests through a sense of obligation to our loved one to resolve on their behalf the loose threads of their life that pain us so. We may try to make peace with our loved one over past conflicts. We might talk to them in our prayers or even try doing things like writing letters to our deceased loved one or using techniques of psychodrama and role playing. Whether you believe your loved one can hear these things is a personal matter of faith, but going through the steps of saying what you need to say will help you clarify the issues and bring you in touch with what you need to do to free yourself from guilt. Some survivors identify all the things they wish they had done more of for their deceased loved one. They may rectify their guilt by doing these very things for others who are still alive. Incorporating the lessons we learned through our relationships with our loved one and applying it to others in our lives is one of the highest honors we can give to our loved one.

Some survivors go even further. They find themselves taking on their deceased loved one's hurts and angers, possibly even confronting their loved one's adversaries and perpetrators. Survivors may find they are angry at parents for not providing a good enough childhood for the victim, angry at their loved one's spouse for not being a better husband or wife, or angry at anyone who was less than kind to their deceased loved one. We may feel a strong need to say our piece, and our loved one's piece, to make peace. Sometimes the role of survivors is to serve as the victim's voice, but it is a role that calls for extreme caution. You need to be crystal clear about how your loved one's issues might also be your own. By taking up our loved one's issues with others, we may also be disowning responsibility for confronting issues that really are our own.

Loss and tragedy can permanently change our values and priorities. We may find ourselves choosing people over money, children over work, church over sleeping in late on Sundays, or "Little House On The Prairie" over "Friday the 13th." We may find that we no longer have room in our lives for jobs that are not fulfilling, relationships that are not honest, entertainment that is violent, or people who are abusive. We may find ourselves pulling old dreams out of the closet to wear or taking the time to do things that we may have brushed off in the past.

It is good to transform trauma and crisis into clarity about our values and beliefs and use it to inspire us to pursue our true works of love. However, it is critical that we re-define our self-measures of success accordingly so we do not end up flunking ourselves when we are really doing A+ work towards our new priorities. For example, if you decide that right now, advocating for justice is the most important thing in your life, then you will need to adjust your normal expectations to accommodate for the time and energy that the battle for justice can involve.

The time and energy involved in grief and the pursuit of justice are tremendous and it is not uncommon to put large portions of our lives on hold. Or, if you decide that spending time with your kids is more important than working weekends, you also need to adjust your financial goals instead of kicking yourself on payday and muttering, "God, I must be losing my edge. I used to bring in more money than this."

Overcoming guilt, shame, and failure is generally not a one-time event since these feelings have a tendency to wax and wane in concert with other issues we are dealing with in our day-to-day life. It is not uncommon for survivors to deal with their guilt, believe it is resolved, feel relieved, only to have it re-emerge at a later date to be addressed anew. The important concept to recognize is that if we address our guilt when it arises, that guilt tends to be less intense and crippling the next time it arises. If we can find the courage to face our guilt, we generally will find that it gets easier instead of harder to resolve each time it crops up. We may also find that dealing with guilt related to our loved one's murder helps us address guilt that we may harbor in other aspects of our lives.

There are many proactive ways of attending to our feelings of guilt and failure. One, talk back to your guilt. Remind yourself that your loved one is dead, not because of anything you did or did not do. They are dead because of the choices and actions of a murderer. As individuals, we are not responsible for the free will of someone else's evil, especially after that evil will has already been executed. Some things simply are not up to us to change. Remind yourself of where your power and responsibility end and someone else's begins. Let the murderer be the one to account for their acts, not you.

Two, talk to others who you trust to be understanding and nonjudgmental. Shame and guilt grow in climates of secrecy and isolation. Expressing your feelings of guilt is a major step to relinquishing that guilt. Other people can serve as compassionate and healthy reflective mediums. They can help us re-align our levels of self-compassion with the compassion that others feel for us. Talking to other survivors can be particularly powerful because they can better relate to what we are experiencing since they have "been there" themselves. When listening to other survivors speak of their feelings of guilt and responsibility, we often find ourselves thinking and saying exactly the words that we most need to hear. Helping and lending emotional support to others during hard times also has the advantage of bolstering our own good feelings about ourselves, which will further help us to cope with our feelings of guilt and failure.

Three, judge yourself compassionately based upon what information and options you had relating to the murder, not the information that has been discovered since the investigation. Ask yourself if your best friend were dealing with your circumstances and your guilt, what would you tell them? Consider extending this same level of compassion to yourself. Understand that the hardest part of giving up your feelings of guilt, failure, and shame is embracing your vulnerabilities and letting go of your vanity, pride, and inflated sense of power and control.

CHAPTER TEN

Forgiveness and Redemption

Just because your loved one was murdered, does not mean that forgiveness and redemption of a murderer have to become one of your life's missions. There are others to carry out this calling. If you are one of them, you will hear the calling and discover what you need to do. Embracing the spirit of forgiveness does not require that we make a judgment about whether the murderer is worthy or not worthy of being forgiven. We do not have to make a direct declaration of forgiveness to the murderer. We do not have to utter the words, "I forgive you." There is no sin in turning the responsibility of forgiveness over to a higher power. Even Jesus turned over forgiveness to God while he was dying on the cross. He did not reassure his slayers that they were forgiven. He shouted, "Father, forgive them for they know not what they do." Jesus was right, they know not what they do. If the murderer had the capacity to fully comprehend and care about the trauma, grief, and pain they inflicted, it would have been impossible for them to commit the murder. Helping the murderer develop the capacity for compassion is not the survivor's job unless you have a compelling reason or drive to make it your job. In most instances, the victim's survivors are simply too close to the pain and the loss to assume the role of spiritual mentor to the murderer.

None of us has the power to look into the heart of someone else and know for sure whether redemption and remorse are real or whether forgiveness is deserved. Most murderers are masters of deception and manipulation, and their evil thrives on the trust and forgiveness of naive and innocent people. Forgiving those who do not deserve it, have not asked for it, and repeatedly betray it, is throwing one of God's greatest gifts into the sewer. If a murderer is truly committed to walking the path of redemption and experiencing the pain that true compassion and remorse would entail for them, they will walk it with or without your forgiveness. The murderer's redemption does not have to involve you unless you want it to.

At least once during their healing journey, most murder victim survivors are called upon to contemplate forgiveness of the murderer. The impetus sometimes comes from our heart, sometimes from our spiritual beliefs, and other times from the suggestions of other people. Some survivors believe that forgiveness is between them and the murderer, some believe it is between the victim and the murderer, and others believe it is between the murderer and their own higher power. Either way, forgiveness definitely has its place. When placed deservingly, it can be a new beginning. Foregiveness can be peace. When placed undeservingly, it becomes an opportunity for cruel people to hurt more people.

Forgiveness can be a healing tool, but it can also be hurtful if we demand it of ourselves unconditionally as if it were an obligation to the murderer. The power and meaning of forgiveness is diminished when it is treated as a decision or event instead of a process, or a moral mandate instead of something that the offender requests and the offended considers. Consideration of forgiveness may entail a deep exploration of the murderer's circumstances, acts of restitution, feelings and beliefs, or it may entail words such as "Go to hell!" flying out of the survivor's mouth quicker than projectile vomit. Both reactions are understandable. Both reactions are respectable.

If you choose not to forgive the murderer, there will always be people to tell you that you are wrong. You might hear things such as: "You have to forgive him to save your own soul." "It even says in the Bible, we should forgive." "You have given yourself up to vengeance." "Your pain won't go away until you forgive." "Try to have some compassion for what makes a person grow up to be a killer." "But she is not the same woman that killed your son. Five years in prison have changed her." "He says he's sorry. Can't you just forgive." "Your forgiveness will help inspire him to find God. How can that be bad?" If you choose to forgive the murderer, there will always be people to tell you that you should not have. You might hear things such as: "If it had been my sister who was strangled, I would have stood up to the bastard and shown him what it is liked to be choked to death." "You've crossed the line from martyrdom to idiocy." "Any self-respecting individual would never forgive the killer of their child." "Your bleeding heart loves the murderer more than your own child." You might even catch yourself thinking some of these things yourself. Dismiss the judgments and criticisms. They can only whittle away at your self-esteem, making it harder for you to consider clearly the process of forgiveness and whether it is a road that you need to take. There are valid reasons for choosing to forgive or not to forgive. Your forgiveness is at your discretion and no one else's. Forgiveness is meaningless if it is not sincerely felt. Some survivors sincerely want to forgive, but sincerely cannot.

Some survivors choose to forgive not for the murderer but for themselves. They believe forgiving will release them from the emotional pain. Murder leaves some survivors feeling so betrayed they can no longer trust any of their fellow human beings. Murder leaves some survivors with such an overwhelming sense of loss, they find they can no longer give, or they resent the gifts, celebrations, and rites of passage of others. It is hard to celebrate the birth or wedding of someone else's child when you are intensely grieving the loss of your own. Grief and murder can leave survivors with such an intense case of "could've, should've, would've" that they cannot free themselves of guilt and self-blame, and they begin to see everything in life in terms of what should happen. They lose tolerance for the innocent mistakes of others. Murder leaves some survivors with such rage that they feel angry all the time. These are all signs that we are holding onto something that is hurting us and possibly hurting others. Forgiveness can be an incredibly powerful means of letting go of this pain, but it is not the sole means. If you are exploring forgiveness as part of your healing and get stuck, it could mean that forgiving is not the best way to help yourself at this time.

Some survivors believe that if they go to the core of their pain and forgive, all the pain will go away. So they seek out the murderer and make that desperate leap off the cliff into forgiveness, not knowing for certain whether they will reach the other side or what they will find if they do. Some find that forgiving the murderer did soften their anger and rage and brought them the peace they needed to reclaim their own lives. Others find themselves disillusioned because the magic words, "I forgive you" did not end the pain. Others find themselves frozen at the cliff's edge too afraid or too angry to jump, asking themselves, "If I can't forgive, what hope of finding peace do I have? And, if I place my faith in my forgiveness and later discover that my forgiveness has fallen prey to an insincere apology, what hope will I have of ever trusting my forgiving nature again?"

Forgiving does not necessarily have to entail the murderer apologizing and the survivor accepting the apology with words of forgiveness. Forgiveness does not mean that murder is okay with us. It does not mean forgetting what happened to our loved one. You will never forget. Forgetting is a passive act largely outside of our control. Forgiving is a conscious choice not to continually remind ourselves of the ways we have been hurt and betrayed by others, so that *we* do not have to endure repeatedly the emotional pain that comes with these thoughts. Forgiveness of this variety is not an all-or-nothing process. It cannot be rushed. Forgiving cannot be feigned. Forgiving is simply a choice to try to change the emotional energy we bask in everyday. If we pre-occupy our emotions by recounting our past hurts, losses, and betrayals over and over and over again, there will be less energy left to count the blessings that come our way each day. We are at risk for developing very bad attitudes, not just toward the murderer, but toward life in general. Not pre-occupying ourselves with the murderer's betrayals and violations of humanity is hard. Our loved one's absence from this earth is a constant reminder. Our grief is a constant reminder. Many survivors find that turning over the matter of forgiveness to God helps them accomplish the goal of choosing not to repeatedly remind themselves of what the murderer deserves and why. From the survivor's standpoint, the murderer has very little to do with the process. The well-being of the forgiver is the focus here.

Forgiving the murderer is not a pre-requisite to healing and it is certainly not the only type of forgiveness worth exploring. Sometimes the key to healing is doing just the opposite of forgiving the murderer. The journey to forgiveness often starts by placing every drop of blame and anger for your loved one's murder squarely on the shoulders of the killer, so you can first and foremost forgive yourself, forgive the rest of the world, and forgive God for not preventing the murder. We may even need to forgive our loved one for falling victim to violence, for being too nice, or for not taking heed and leaving the gate open for evil to walk in and steal their life. Start your journey of forgiveness with those who bear the least responsibility for your loved one's death instead of the person most responsible. Taking forgiveness this far is sometimes far enough for survivors to find the peace that was stolen by the murderer.

Sometimes we try to take the journey of forgiveness backwards, from those most responsible to least responsible, because of our guilt and fear. We forgive those we fear in hopes that our gift will soothe the killer's violence, offer us more safety, and put it to sleep. The survivor may blame themselves for failing to prevent the murder to avoid confronting the perpetrator; for example, the abused child who shows the abusing parent more love than the non-abusing parent in hopes that their love and favor will somehow stop the abuse. Sometimes we forgive the killer to try to relieve our own sense of guilt. We rationalize that if we can forgive the unforgivable, then it will be easier to forgive ourselves. Sometimes we contemplate forgiveness simply because it is the only part of the whole damn situation that we have control over. Sometimes we withhold forgiveness for the very same reason. If you do choose to forgive, it is important to sort out your feelings about yourself from your feelings about the murderer and to be clear about why you are forgiving. If you forgive yourself first, your motives and expectations will be much clearer to you when you broach forgiving the perpetrator.

Many want to forgive because they believe their religion mandates that they forgive. When they find that they cannot forgive without betraying their honesty and sincerity, they are thrust into a spiritual dilemma. "Forgive us our trespasses as we forgive those who trespass against us." The Lord's Prayer does not say we have to forgive all wrongs that are done to us. The Prayer expresses the need to balance our shortcomings, our compassion, and our willingness to forgive. It is asking us to make the leap from understanding ourselves to understanding others and back again. If I want to be forgiven for stepping on your toe, then I should be willing to muster the understanding to forgive someone else for stepping on mine. Likewise, if I forgive you of murder, then I can hope for my own soul to be forgiven if I ever commit murder. Most survivors are quite comfortable living with the assurance that they will not commit murder. Their moral revulsion to murder makes it unlikely if not impossible for them to commit such a deep violation of life. You do not have to reconcile your values and humanity with those of a heartless killer, especially if it means weaving something into your soul's fabric that does not seem to belong there. Sometimes we are spiritually better off not understanding the compulsions of evil that lure a person to kill. Sometimes it is best merely to be aware that such cruelty exists without trying to understand it.

Some survivors consider forgiveness because the murderer apologizes to them and asks for it. Some find comfort in the apology and others find it to be just another emotional dilemma to deal with. When you consider the magnitude of loss that murder entails, the words, "I'm sorry" just echo with emptiness. Not because the apology is or is not sincere, but because the words are not much different than the ones used by a kid apologizing for breaking a window with a baseball. Unlike the broken window, a murderer cannot amend a death. I do not know if our language has words of apology that go deep enough to reach the depth of violation we experience when someone is murdered. Survivors also may have difficulty trusting the sincerity of the apology.

Sometimes convincing others of their remorse is nothing more than another manipulative power trip for the murderer. Is it real, or is it just something the murderer wants to present at the next parole hearing as evidence of their rehabilitation? Is the apology genuine or a con to brag about to their cell mate? Am I supposed to accept the apology, and if I do, what does it mean? The position of receiving an apology is an emotional burden you do not have to carry. You can ignore the apology until you feel ready to respond, or you can say "apology accepted," "I will consider your apology," "apology not accepted," or "good for you, but it changes nothing for me." If the apology is sincere, God and the perpetrator will know and feel the difference. If the apology is not sincere (surprise,

surprise), God and they will know the difference. Forgiveness sought by the perpetrator does not have to involve the survivor at all. The Twelve Steps of Alcoholics Anonymous promotes that perpetrators "seek forgiveness and make amendments except when doing so could cause harm to others." The more a murderer remains a part of your life, the more distress they can cause you. Sincerely sorry people recognize when they are doing you more harm than good for selfish reasons.

Sometimes survivors choose to forgive because there are circumstances that make forgiveness more worthwhile and important to the survivor to pursue. Sometimes the murderer is someone we once knew, loved, and respected, or a member of our own family, such as a child who killed their own sibling or a father who killed the mother of his children. The survivor embarks on the path of forgiveness and redemption with the murderer because they believe it is their duty to bring peace to their family, or to resolve the great emotional conflicts that stem from hating the murderer for what they did, but still loving them anyhow for who they are. Perhaps the survivor believes that if they help save the murderer's soul, it will help bring positive meaning to their loved one's death. Sometimes we choose to forgive because we truly believe the murderer never intended to kill, but rather made some bad choices that resulted in a tragic outcome that traumatized and horrified them too. Sometimes the murderer is sick or mentally ill. Sometimes we choose to forgive because the murderer has said the right words and done the right things to make us want to forgive. Sometimes, even when we want to forgive, the best we can muster is to dissect the murderer and dissect ourselves so that the best of ourselves can forgive the best of them.

Forgiveness involves a whole spectrum of feelings, beliefs, words, and actions. We can explore some of them, all of them, or none of them. Admitting to and dealing with our inability to forgive is much healthier than pretending. If you do forgive and it brings you peace, celebrate it and feel good about yourself. If you cannot forgive, do not want to forgive, and do not see where trying to forgive will bring you any peace or benefit, it simply means that forgiveness of the murderer will not be part of your journey. Peace and healing are not contingent on forgiving the murderer.

There are many other ways to heal.

Many survivors believe that their burning desire for the murderer to feel the pain they created is at odds with the process of forgiveness. "How can I forgive, when all I want is for the murderer to hurt—hurt like their victim hurt, hurt like the victim's parents hurt, hurt like the victim's brothers and sisters hurt, hurt like the victim's child hurt, or best friend hurt?" If we look spiritually at the process of forgiveness, we will see that pain and forgiveness are not mutually exclusive. They go hand in hand. Since the pain that the murder created extends far beyond mere physical pain and into the emotional and spiritual realms, it takes more than physical acts to inflict upon the murderer all the pain they created by taking a life. God's forgiveness is not unconditional. Sincere repentance is required. Sincere repentance requires compassion and a conscience. When we hurt others, our conscience hurts us. A conscience is the only thing that can bring the murderer to fully feel the pain they created. Some survivors, rather than struggling with whether or not to forgive the murderer, turn the issue over to their higher power and pray that the murderer be blessed with a conscience, knowing this will hurt worse than anything they could ever do to the murderer. There are some survivors that go a step further and pray that the murderer be blessed with a conscience and also that they find the strength to endure the pain that conscience brings long enough to follow it all the way to salvation.

The murderer's redemption is not dependent upon your forgiveness. There are organizations and individuals whose mission is to help violent offenders develop compassion and pursue restitution and redemption. If the murderer really does make it through that journey of remorse and feels all the pain they created—good. Their sorry souls will need it. It would be a victory for humanity if every murderer were able to kill the monster within to save the best of themselves. Ultimately, redemption does help make our world a safer, more peaceful place. However, most survivors are too hurt by the losses inflicted by the murderer to celebrate their discovery of a conscience or validate the pain of their remorse.

CHAPTER ELEVEN

The Eclipse of Trauma and Grief

Grief and trauma naturally eclipse one another. All deaths traumatize the living to some degree. Likewise, all trauma involves loss—loss of innocence, loss of safety, loss of self-esteem, loss of trust, loss of limb, loss of functioning, loss of life—loss, loss, loss, and more loss. If trauma survivors fail to grieve their losses, they risk stagnating in their trauma. If the bereaved fail to recognize and address the trauma they have experienced, they risk stagnating in their grief. With most deaths, a partial eclipse occurs between grief and trauma. With murder, grief and trauma are in full eclipse.

Death is rarely okay with those that are left behind to live. Typically, survivors of all deaths are left with some unresolved emotional and spiritual issues. Many of our emotional, psychological, and spiritual reactions to murder are common to all manners of death, and other aspects are unique to murder. Understanding and distinguishing these reactions can prevent trauma and grief from gridlocking into chronic psychological and emotional torment.

Even when we expect someone to die and have prepared for it, death shocks us. Survivors who watch their loved one suffer and die from disease are usually traumatized to some extent by the experience. Parents who have lost a child to a brain tumor may find themselves constantly scanning their remaining children for symptoms. Every eye twitch becomes cause for panic. The violations of nature and disease upon our bodies can be physically horrific just as the injuries inflicted at the hand of another human being are beyond gruesome. There is nothing peaceful about tumor growth, bleeding ulcers, rampant infection, uncontrollable shaking, profuse sweating, vomiting, raging fevers, open sores, brain atrophy, seizures, strokes, and heart attacks. The victims of disease hurt, fear, beg for help, and plead for their lives as murder victims do. Disease victims generally have some indication of what is coming and their survivors have the opportunity to go through it with them—an opportunity often viewed as a mixed blessing, a painful but precious honor. Murder victim survivors often grieve the lost opportunity to comfort their loved one through their suffering and to say goodbye.

Just as survivors of natural deaths might take issue with God, nature, a colony of bacteria, a cluster of cancer cells, the drug pusher, the doctors, the tobacco and alcohol industry, or their loved one for unhealthy lifestyle choices, murder victim survivors take issue with the murderer, the justice system, humanity, and God. Survivors of natural deaths usually experience symptoms of normal grief while the survivors of murders typically endure normal grief combined with symptoms of posttraumatic stress disorder (PTSD). The combination can become chronic and debilitating if healthy ways of addressing the emotional and spiritual wounds are not found.

For murder victim survivors, the trauma of death is intensified by the dark elements of violence and evil involved, the introduction of a perpetrator, the secondary victimization by the law enforcement and justice systems, and the gross violation of basic and sacred human trusts and values. Murder is about someone being hurt and tormented until they escape their attacker by death. Death by disease is about escaping a weary and sickly body.

The trauma experienced by the victim before their death becomes intertwined with the trauma experienced by the survivor after death. There are many, many murder victim survivors suffering from severe posttraumatic stress disorder because they were witnesses to the murder: children scared for their lives who hid under the bed and endured the sights and sounds of people they love being beaten, shot, raped, and tortured—truly powerless to protect them; wives who tried to pull the raging attacker off their already unconscious husbands; or brothers outnumbered in a gang attack who could do nothing to help each other. Survivors can even be traumatized by the murder if they did not witness it. Fears or memories about our loved one's death can play like broken records in our heads. We become immersed in the cruel and relentless violence of their murders. Since so many murder victim survivors do not witness the murder, friends and professionals often fail to recognize how at-risk murder victim survivors are for developing chronic symptoms of posttraumatic stress disorder. Witnessing the murder or its aftermath is enough to change a person forever. Murder victim survivors react in ways similar to other types of trauma survivors such as war veterans, disaster survivors, child abuse survivors, or rape survivors.

Murder burns a river of horror and outrage right across our beings. The river leaves us thirsty for the peace that always seems to be on the other side. As we search for a way to cross, we are tempted to quench our thirst by drinking of the river's poison. We drink and fall in over and over again until we learn what the river really is, where it comes from, and where it goes. The river remains and our thirst remains until we find our way to the other side of trauma and grief.

Posttraumatic stress disorder manifests in varied ways such as flashbacks, nightmares, dissociation, isolation, obsessive thoughts, depression, withdrawal, emotional numbness, hyper-vigilance, and emotional outbursts out of proportion to the situation at hand. The symptoms of posttraumatic stress disorder can be dichotomous and contradictory by nature. Some murder victim survivors are so overwhelmed that they cannot get their minds around the murder enough to talk about it, while other survivors cannot seem to talk about anything else. Some murder victim survivors are too depressed to get out of bed and go to work, while others plunge themselves into work coming home only to sleep. Some survivors find they cannot emotionally tolerate any violence, whether it be in movies, news, or books, while others do not seem interested in anything but murder- and death-related materials. Some survivors become overly sensitive and reactive, while others become numb and devoid of feelings.

If left unaddressed, posttraumatic stress disorder can lead to other mental health disorders such as chronic depression and anxiety, or drive survivors to seek escape in unhealthy ways, such as turning to drugs, alcohol, compulsive sex, compulsive eating, or other dysfunctional cycles. Recognizing the symptoms and understanding that your reactions are normal to your circumstances are the first step to minimizing the impact of posttraumatic stress disorder on the quality of your life and ability to function.

The most common symptom of posttraumatic stress disorder is the relentless re-experiencing of the trauma. The diagnostic manual of criteria for psychological conditions, the DSM-IV, describes the symptoms as *"Recurrent and intrusive distressing recollections of the event, including images, thoughts, or perceptions"* (American Psychiatric Association, DSM-IV, pp. 427-428). Recurrent recollections are also an important part of normal grieving. At times, the remembering involved with normal grief can be very intrusive and very distressing, especially during the more acute phases of grief. We remember something about our loved one, we remember our loved one is dead, we re-experience the surge of emotions that came with learning they were dead, and react anew as if a brand new heart is breaking. The re-dawning of grief looks a lot like the recurrent memories of trauma victims. Both can be gut-wrenching and both take a long time to percolate through our beings.

With murder, memories of our loved one become involuntarily wed not only to our grief reactions, but also to images of murder. Images of murder can be sights, smells, sounds, or other sensations surrounding the murder that we actually experienced, witnessed, imagined, or observed secondhand through photographs or verbal descriptions. Every time we think of our loved one, we think of the murder. Instead of our memories triggering our feelings about our loved one, bringing them closer to us, we end up experiencing our feelings about the murder and the murderer. Our memories get kidnapped, tainted, vandalized, and desecrated by the murderer. How can you even begin to grieve when you cannot separate your memories of your loved one from the atrocities of murder? The trauma of the murder holds its victims hostage in their graves.

Another symptom of posttraumatic stress disorder is *"intense psychological distress or physiological reactivity on exposure to internal or external cues that symbolize or resemble an aspect of the traumatic event"* (American Psychiatric Association, DSM-IV, pp. 427-428). Even with "normal" deaths and uncomplicated grief, there will be cues that trigger grief reactions, especially at first, such as Christmas, birthdays, anniversaries of death, a piece of mail addressed to the deceased, entering a bedroom, passing a funeral procession or cemetery, or seeing someone that simply looks a lot like your deceased loved one. For murder victim survivors, the cues evoke much more than grief. Some survivors experience intense anger when they see people that remind them of the murderer. Some murder victim survivors find they cannot watch television after the murder of their loved one. The violence in the news and on television triggers intense emotional reactions and flashbacks, plunging them back into the heat of their own loved one's murder. We live in a society that uses murder for entertainment and reports murders widely in the news. Avoiding the topic of murder in our media-driven society is nearly impossible. The trauma is like a sliver that is repeatedly driven deeper and deeper until it becomes infamed and cannot heal.

Memories of our deceased loved one can become cues that trigger distressing posttraumatic reactions. "For two solid years every time I thought of my brother, I also thought of his murderer. Thoughts of the murderer led me to bitter outrage. Even in my own mind, my brother had been inextricably linked to this putrid evil person and his putrid evil act. I didn't want to think about murdering pukes. I wanted to think about my brother. I did not want to experience rage. I wanted to experience remembrance and love. Not only did the murderer take my brother's life, he also stole his memory right out of my own head! It is like the seed of some evil entity was planted inside me to torment me and keep me from my brother. The murderer never touched me, but he most certainly raped my mind. I hate that I can remember the murderer's face better than my own brother's." Memories cannot really be stolen, but they can be buried or overshadowed. It can take years to unearth our memories of our loved one from beneath the trauma of murder.

Posttraumatic stress disorder can manifest as "recurrent distressing dreams of the event" or "feeling as if the traumatic event were recurring (includes a sense of reliving the experience- illusions, hallucinations, and dissociative flashback episodes, including those that occur on awakening or when intoxicated)" (American Psychiatric Association, DSM-IV, pp. 427-428). Some survivors experience repeated nightmares about the murder and/or the murderer. Some survivors feel haunted. Some just cannot get the images out of their head. Every time they close their eyes, they see blood and gore. Other survivors report experiences of feeling like they have just been notified of the murder, even though they have been aware of the murder for years.

Posttraumatic stress disorder can involve *"persistent avoidance of stimuli associated with the trauma and numbing of general responsiveness* (American Psychiatric Association, DSM-IV, pp. 427-428). Avoidance and numbing boil down to shutting down emotionally and retreating from trauma, grief, and life. Avoidance can take many forms. Some survivors suffer from memory blocks. They do not remember being notified of their loved one's death, they cannot remember identifying their loved one's body, or they do not remember what they were doing the day of the murder. Other survivors may retreat from anything that reminds them of the murder. They even avoid thoughts of their loved one to protect themselves from the unwanted intrusions of murder's darkness. Survivors may avoid talking about their loved one. They take down pictures and reminders of their loved one. They avoid grieving to avoid feeling vulnerable. They avoid activities they once did with their loved one or retreat from family activities that used to include their loved one. Some survivors are even traumatized out of their own homes to avoid reminders of the murder. This is especially true if the murder occurred in the survivor's home. Some survivors find themselves in the precarious situation of not wanting to part with the home their loved one lived in, but also being emotionally unable to handle living there themselves.

Survivors may lose interest in activities they once enjoyed or they may dump their life dreams. Survivors may even become emotionally frozen and numb to avoid feeling the pain their loved one's murder left them to bear. They may escape into drugs and alcohol and find themselves lost. Unfortunately, when we swallow our grief and anger instead of feeling and expressing it when we need to, we dull our ability to experience other aspects of ourselves as well, such as joy, pleasure, and intimacy.

Posttraumatic stress disorder may involve *"persistent symptoms of increased arousal"* (American Psychiatric Association, DSM-IV, pp. 427-428). Survivors may become hyper vigilant—guarding themselves, their homes, and their loved ones from perceived threats. They may not sleep well because they feel compelled to guard the house. They may be less tolerant and have angry outbursts out of proportion to the circumstances. Anger and rage over the murder can seep out in response to minor sources of anger or irritation. Innocent mistakes and small infractions of ideal conduct may be perceived as major threats and violations. Little betrayals need to be separated and put into perspective as triggers or reminders of the "ultimate" betrayal of murder. Survivors may find it hard to relax, going through every day revving their anger and fear, ready to race, with nowhere to go. Many survivors report that they cannot concentrate long enough to sit and watch a movie, read a magazine article, do their homework, or organize their work on the job. Even survivors who once were very even-keeled and moderately tempered find that since their loved one was murdered they are unpredictable, discontent, and lose control of their emotions easily.

The goal with normal grief is eventually to be able to remember your loved one without it always being an upsetting or distressing experience. The goal is to be able to enjoy happy memories without feeling sad or angry or guilty. You get used to the fact that they are dead so you do not have to go through the whole grief response every single time you are reminded of your loved one. The only way to accomplish this is to give yourself time to remember and grieve as you need. Even with healthy grieving, there will be times—10, 20, and even 30 years down the line—when grief catches us anew.

Healing from the trauma of murder entails reclaiming your loved one's memories, reclaiming the meaning of their life, and reclaiming the meaning of their death from the murderous act that was perpetrated against them. "Reclaiming" your loved one is a conscious task that initially involves the practice of thought stopping. Choose a topic and think about it for five minutes. When you notice thoughts about anything else entering your head, stop and restart your thinking about the chosen topic. Now, think about your loved one. When intrusive thoughts related to the murder start coming up, stop your thoughts and say, "No, I'm not going there today. That dark place of cruelty and gore is for the murderer, not for me and my loved one." Then, start your thoughts over in a better place. Keep repeating this exercise in thought stopping until you are capable of thinking about your loved one and only your loved one, or any other pleasant image you have invited into your mind. Treat thoughts of the murderer like you would a door-to-door snake oil salesman. Simply show them to the door and then carry on with your business.

Another approach to divorcing thoughts of your loved one from thoughts of the murderer is "talking" directly to your loved one in your thoughts instead of just thinking about them. The direct dialogue makes the encounter more exclusive between you and your loved one, and that can help push intrusive thoughts into the background. It is like having a conversation with one person in a crowded room. As you focus on the single person, everyone else fades into the background.

Creative expression can also help us learn to focus on one set of thoughts and screen out another. We can draw pictures symbolizing our loved ones, portraits of them, or scenarios depicting their death as a passage into a more beautiful realm instead of a passage through hell. The process of art involves a lot of repetition with each brush stroke and every line. The repetition is mantric like a meditation or prayer. We pour ourselves into our creations. The process of creating imbeds our art into our psyches. If you look at and work on a piece of art long enough, you will see it when you close eyes. Art is one means of replacing the agonizing images of murder with images of peace and spiritual victory. Instead of seeing my brother burned to death in a fire, I created images of him being spiritually borne into a ring of exuberant and fiery energy and lifted by winged dovers in the ribbons of a rainbow. I am now, finally, able to think about my brother's death without seeing tortuous images.

It is healthy to separate your loved one's death from their murder. The key to distinguishing the victim's death from their murder is faith—faith that your loved one's experience of death and the afterlife is based solely upon the goodness of their souls, the love they brought to this life, and the love they take with them into the spiritual realm; faith in the healing graces that any pain that followed your loved one from this realm to the next was soothed and healed; and faith that the murderer will be made to own the murder and suffer the pain of their crimes against humanity, if not in this world, then most certainly in the next. As for the survivors left here in this life aching and hurting from the horror of the murder, we do continue to bear the consequences of the murder until we find ways to let go of the despair and harness the rage so we do not waste our life's energy bearing a burden that belongs solely to the murderer.

In order to have times when you do not think of the murder or the murderer, you need to allow yourself times when you can. Give yourself permission to think of the murder and vent until you are too tired to say anything more. Do it in a face-to-face conversation, do it on the phone, in email, a chat room, with a pen pal, with a support group of other murder victim survivors, with just paper and pen, or a paintbrush and canvas—anything. All that matters is that you do it. Get the toxins of murder out of you. You need to say your piece if you ever expect to have peace. Learning when to give the murder mental and emotional time and when to deny the murder time is a way to reclaim power over your thoughts, memories, and feelings from the murderer.

Trauma and grief come in layers. We have a tendency to work through a layer and feel like we have reclaimed our lives again, forgetting that there is still more work for us to do. Then, unexpectedly, the survivor is thrown back into crisis by re-experiencing the trauma in some way—a nightmare or a flashback. Whether it be in the form of locking doors, throwing pots and pans in a rage, or not being able to get out of bed one day, crisis is what our minds and emotions do to force us to deal with something. Although it is distressing, crisis serves a purpose.

Re-experiencing the trauma is a sign that your psyche is still screaming for something or still has something to scream about. The more you try to ignore and suppress the trauma you are suffering from, the more you will be intruded upon by heightened emotional responses and uninvited re-experiencing of the trauma. The psyche periodically needs to revisit the crisis to protest, "No, no, no. None of this is okay. It will never be okay." Perhaps it is nothing more than needing the pain and loss to be recognized and validated again. It is okay for you to go back to revisit the trauma when you need to. You made it through the reality the first time, you are stronger now and will survive the vestiges that trauma has left for you to contend with again.

The grief and trauma of murder leave us with so much to work out spiritually, emotionally, mentally, and socially that there is no way we can chew through it all in a single bite. It is too much. How can you work through your despair at the same time you are still working through numbness and denial? You cannot, so you work through the trauma and loss twice. How can you work through the impact of the murder on your relationships if you have not even worked through your own feelings about murder? You cannot, so you go through it a couple more times. How can you open the door to venting and expressing your rage when you need to be ready to stand face-to-face with a murderer in a courtroom without losing composure? How can you work through your feelings of loss when you have not realized all your losses? You cannot, so you go through it each time a new loss is realized. We do not realize our losses in an instant; we realize them over the years. After five years, the list of what you have lost to the murder will likely be longer than it was at one year. You need to validate your feelings and experiences no matter how old they are. If a friend of yours had a child who was murdered today, how would you deal with them? You need to give yourself every bit of that same compassion and validation.

The tragedy of murder is kept alive in the survivor's heart for a long, long time—for most survivors, their entire lives. By necessity, the murder stays alive until the pursuit of justice is complete. The journey to justice demands composure and often works contrary to the process of healing from trauma and grief. The quest for justice sometimes demands obsession. Many survivors will say that, in retrospect, they did not even begin to heal until the trial and conviction were behind them and they finally had the opportunity to confront the murderer and deliver an impact statement in court. Most survivors, by necessity, pack-up their grief, carry it on their backs, and do not really take it out until the journey to justice has ended through either resolution or exhaustion.

If the survivor thinks of their loved one and it is still all about the murderer, the survivor is still dealing with the trauma and has not fully begun to grieve. To grieve would be to think about your loved one fondly and longingly. When the survivor thinks of their loved one and it is finally all about them and not the murderer, the survivor has entered a purer stage of grieving. If the survivor thinks of their loved one and smiles instead of cries, they have touched shore on the other side of grief.

The first goal in homicidal grief is being able to think about your murdered loved one without thinking about the murder or the murderer. Everytime you can do this, you are reclaiming yet another connection with your loved one from the shadow of murder. Then, the next step is getting to a point where you can think about your loved one without it being a distressing experience, which is typically one of the first milestones in normal grief. Most survivors eventually have times when they are able to meet both challenges, but they are not necessarily able to pull it off at will all the time.

There will always be times when you cry. There will always be times when you feel angry and horrified about your loved one's murder. There will always be a struggle to keep perspective by sorting out homicidal grief issues from normal grief issues. There will always be misunderstandings if others expect survivors of murder victims to grieve normally and to let go of the complex issues raised by murder without processing them on an emotional and spiritual level. Likewise, there will be misunderstandings if murder victim survivors forget that grief is not uniquely theirs and that only aspects of their grief are unique to their circumstances. Surviving the aftermath of murder involves sensitizing survivors and others in a position to help to the issues unique to homicidal grief.

CHAPTER TWELVE

The Road to Justice:
Investigating a Murder

The first step on the road to justice is recognizing that a murder has been committed. Murder is not always obvious. It masquerades as accidents and suicides. The victim of a fall or a jump looks a lot like the victim of a push. The wounds from an accidental gunshot look a lot like the wounds from an intentional gunshot. The victim whose body is never found looks a lot like someone who has run away. Murder is uncomfortably easy to cover up and overlook. Sometimes, all that is ever known for certain is that someone is dead or missing.

Deaths in our society are routinely processed and sifted through a purview of professionals such as law enforcement officers, paramedics, doctors, funeral directors, and medical examiners, who are trained and paid to attend to the details of death. They are required by law to look closely at every death for signs of foul play that might warrant the next layer of investigation. Federal and state governments have policies, statutes, and protocols in place that lay out how various types of deaths should be handled and investigated. Suicides, shootings, fire fatalities, and other traumatic, suspicious, or unexplained deaths are usually followed by an autopsy and at least a brief investigation. Ideally, the investigation stays open and active until the victim is identified, the cause and manner of death are determined, and murder is either definitively ruled out or the murderer is identified and prosecuted.

Unfortunately, this is not how it always goes. If one of the responding professionals fails to do their job conscientiously or if the murderer's knowledge and skills in forensic deception exceed the effort or investigative prowess of the professionals responding to the death, someone gets away with murder. Often professionals such as police or medical examiners are the ones to initiate a homicide investigation, but on many occasions the victim's survivors notify police that a homicide investigation is needed. Those who are trained and paid to know what to look for sometimes do not launch an investigation intensive enough to identify or arrest a suspect. They may overlook key pieces of evidence. Do not make the mistake of assuming that the police and medical examiners will know better than you if something was amiss regarding your loved one's death. Survivors are in a better position to notice details others cannot. Survivors knew the victim, their lifestyle, the people they associated with, and their habits better than the investigators. You do not have to be a detective or a medical examiner to smell foul play. You only need to care enough to look, notice, and take action.

With every moment a murder goes uninvestigated, the slimmer the chances are of identifying a suspect and proving murder. As the sun rises and falls, evidence changes hands, gets contaminated, weathered, or lost while the murderer puts distance, deception, and disguise between themselves and their murderous act. Evidence loses credibility in the courtroom every time it is handled or passed by a different person. Memories of significant events fade. The sooner you act on your concerns, the better.

A tremendous burden is placed on survivors when the job of uncovering and resolving the murder of their loved one is left to them. But the reality is, many times the job becomes theirs by default. Investigators eventually move on to new cases that compete with old unresolved cases for time, energy, and investigative resources. Homicide investigation is not a first-come, first-served type of business. All too often, survivors are left to hold the stinging cold reality of an unresolved murder for the rest of their lives.

Separating feelings of grief from intuitive feelings about how your loved one died can be difficult. Manner of death has a huge bearing on the issues and feelings survivors grapple with internally. Although the end result is the same, your loved one is dead. It is important to know whether your loved one was murdered, committed suicide, or died accidentally. Although grief inevitably becomes wrapped around aspects of your loved one's death, it is not right for you or anybody else to discount your thoughts, suspicions, or intuitions just because you are grieving. The more intertwined your grief is with the circumstances of death, the more important it becomes to confirm or disconfirm your concerns. Despite what others may insinuate, you have a right to a reasonable investigation and the best available explanation of cause and manner of death.

The first clue to murder may only be a feeling that something is very wrong—something beyond the mere fact of death, something evil. The circumstances, the timeframes, the people, the statements swirling around your loved one's death, just are not making sense. Everything inside your gut is saying, "Someone is lying!" Or perhaps no one is saying much at all and the silence is speaking louder than the words. The questions of murder whisper persistently in the aftermath of death. "If it was suicide, why weren't the prints from his bare feet on the chair that he supposedly stood on to reach the noose?" "If she drowned accidentally while skinny dipping alone in the pond, then where are the clothes she took off before going into the water?" Your questions and observations warrant serious consideration. These questions and observations may be the keystones to justice.

Recognizing that a murder has occurred inevitably involves piercing the veil of shock and denial that surrounds the newly bereaved like a bubble carrying them with mercy through the first wakes of grief. Survivors vary greatly in their level of attentiveness, confidence, and level of functioning, especially during the initial phases of grief. Sometimes the shock and denial are so thick that even the hard and sharp facts of a blatant murder are not enough to pierce the bubble. When there is no more room for pain, survivors may reject without consideration anything that threatens to cause them more pain. It is impossible to fully comprehend the reality of murder until emotionally we are ready to handle the painful flood of emotions that such a realization would bring. Shock and denial can make the plausibility of murder slow to emerge. Nobody wants to believe murder really happens, especially to someone they love and cherish, or at the hand of someone they know.

Piercing the veil of denial entails a willingness to look at the facts and circumstances and consider all plausible manners of death, including murder. Once the possibility of murder dawns on a survivor, they are thrust into the role of piercing the shock and denial of others, such as family members, friends, or even police. For many survivors going to the police with their concerns is the next step toward justice, and for others it is going to family members and friends whom they expect to share their interest in finding the truth about their loved one's death.

Before making disclosures to the police, you may want to consider how and when your family members will learn of the murder investigation if you do not tell them first. Do you want family to find out there is an active murder investigation when the police come knocking on their door to ask a few questions? Or, do you want them to learn their loved one's death was a homicide when they read it in the newspaper? There really is no good time to tell someone that their friend or family member may have been murdered. There is no good time to ask, "Do you know of any reason why someone would want to hurt your child, your sibling, your parent, or your friend?" It is important to consider the potential reactions and mental health implications for other family members. The possibility of violent retaliation against the suspect is always a concern when breaking the news to people who are prone to demonstrations of rage. Suicide can be a concern when breaking the news to someone prone to depression or internalized guilt. The best you can do is try to arrange a supportive, safe, non-confrontational setting, where individuals can express their initial reactions without judgment.

Even when survivors raise their suspicions and concerns carefully, the reactions of others can be unpredictable and downright shocking. There will be people who get angry at even the suggestion that someone they know might be a murder suspect, or that someone may have wanted their loved one dead. Because they do not like the insinuation, they react as if the investigation is wrong. They view the investigation as a personal insult instead of a search for truth that will vindicate the innocent—both living and dead. Survivors may encounter others who dishonor the victim with indifference. There may be others still who take the murder so personally that they believe that justice should belong to them alone and be exacted before the evidence of truth has the opportunity to unfold before a jury. Do not be bound by someone else's aversion to the truth. If you have concerns and suspicions, go to the police and insist on a proper investigation. Failure to take the death of another human being seriously enough to investigate it thoroughly is not only an insult against the victim, it is an insult against all humanity. Lives are not disposable.

No matter how survivors conduct themselves, they will be regarded as emotionally charged and prejudiced. There is nothing you as a survivor can do to change this reality. Be aware of the bias, be honest about it, and be proud of the fact that you care enough to act on behalf of the victim. Survivors advocating for justice need to be prepared to clarify for the police, the public, or anyone implying their interest and involvement in the case is inappropriate, that requesting and expecting a thorough investigation is not the same as making unsubstantiated accusations. Sharing information with police and requesting an investigation are what any responsible citizen should do if they have concerns regarding the manner of someone's death. Be careful not to muddy the distinction between advocate of justice and fanatical accuser with inflammatory behavior. Although extreme reactions are understandable, words of outrage and threats of vengeance do nothing to gain positive interest in your loved one's case. Survivors are wise to avoid openly expressing impassioned accusations.

Authorities may respond to the survivor's intensity by questioning their motives or discrediting them due to their extreme emotionality before they have even heard all the survivor has to say. Survivor's concerns may be written off as an unhealthy grief reaction. As part of a criminal defense strategy, survivors are often accused of needing a perpetrator to blame for their grief and losses because they cannot face the facts of their loved one's death. There are people such as insensitive defense attorneys, disinterested policemen, or supporters of the murderer that will attempt to turn the survivor's passionate cry for justice against them. The murderer may later, as part of his or her defense, accuse survivors of biasing witnesses or organizing a vigilante-type conspiracy. Defense attorneys may try to create the perception that the survivor's intensity and passion are wrong. Under most circumstances, it makes sense for survivors to be discreet regarding their suspicions and contacts with police.

Survivors often must decide whether it is better for the case to rally the voices of fellow survivors and supporters or maintain a low profile. There are situations when it may not be wise or appropriate to share your concerns with anyone but the police. Very often the suspect is someone the victim's survivors know and are still in association with, such as an in-law, a blood relative, or a mutual friend. If the murderer is not aware they are suspected, they very well may attempt to maintain ties with the victim's survivors as a means of getting information about the progression of the investigation. In fact, some murderers may be afraid that if they do withdraw from the surviving family, it could raise suspicions. The suspect may even manipulate the situation with feigned grief, sympathy, and supportiveness in an attempt to deepen trust and influence the situation to their own advantage. Should the question of murder arise down the road, the murderer wants it to be emotionally difficult for people to believe that they could be capable of such cruelty and betrayal.

Dealing with a murderer who thinks they have gotten away with it calls for the utmost caution. Murderers have already proven the measures they will use to intimidate and incite fear. Depending where people's loyalties lie, any suspicions you share could make it back to the murder suspect, which could result in them fleeing before the investigation even begins, or retaliating against those who threaten to expose them.

In many cases, there is no one to turn to without risking one's life, especially in areas with high murder rates and poor arrest and conviction outcomes. When murderers are not incarcerated for their crime, witnesses and advocates of justice are placed at risk for harassment, retaliation, and intimidation at the hands of the murderer. If gang or organized crime activity is involved, witnesses may be in danger even if the murderer is in jail.

Survivors are often shocked to discover just how politically and economically driven the investigative process is. When it comes to crime and violence, everyone has a vested interest whether or not they care to recognize this responsibility. Yet, not all murders elicit the same cry for justice. Public interest varies dramatically. The public response to murder can range from the obsession demonstrated in the Washington, D.C., sniper investigation to the indifference seen in the case of a nameless, homeless person who is never identified and never even mentioned in the media.

There are competing incentives and consequences involved in

initiating a murder investigation. For the survivor, the incentive may be justice. For the rookie officer hopeful of promotion, the incentive may be impressing superiors. For homicide detectives and prosecutors, the consequence of opening a murder case may be a heavier workload and a further drain on limited resources. Investing time in difficult cases yields diminishing returns. For other investigators and prosecutors, the murder case may become their primary motivation for going to work each day. The case could become an opportunity for them to chase down a killer in spite of the odds and show the survivors and the community what they are made of. For the community, a murder investigation can mean thousands, perhaps even millions of taxpayer dollars devoted to investigating, prosecuting, and in many instances, publicly defending the case. Trials and appeals are very costly. If justice culminates in conviction, the community can count on thousands of dollars more to house and feed the killers for years to come. Sometimes the effort invested in a case becomes a matter of what the community is willing to pay rather than a matter of justice. The incentives to overlook a murder compete with the incentives to solve one.

The primary incentive for wanting a proper investigation is to honor our loved one, promote public safety, and uphold values of truth, justice, and accountability. Although the list of disincentives for justice can be longer, the incentives to pursue justice come from a deeper place within ourselves and have a longer enduring force. This driving force is a wellspring for survivors to draw from as they continue to motivate those who otherwise do not have a desire to look as closely at the victim's life and death as might be necessary.

The barriers to a proper investigation are many. Some professionals in the law and justice system are operating with vested interests that have nothing to do with justice and public safety. Sometimes our professionals are not empowered enough to command the resources necessary to launch a thorough investigation. Sometimes the professionals are negligent or are simply suffering from job burnout and do not care. Or in some instances, they do care, but are under the rule and command of those who do not. Survivors better the odds of obtaining a thorough investigation every time they express interest in the case and make it known that they are following the progress of the investigation.

Some survivors delay sharing their concerns and suspicions about their loved one's death because nobody else is expressing concerns. They may doubt themselves and ask, "Is it me? Am I having some paranoid grief reaction?" If you seem to be the only one who has concerns and suspicions about your loved one's death, it makes it all the more imperative that you raise them. If you do not, who will? Being the first one to utter, "Oh my God, this could be murder" is very hard to do, especially if everyone else is proceeding as if no crime has been committed. The word "murder" is a bell that cannot be un-rung, and the process that follows that discordant clank can take on a life of its own very quickly.

Murders and murder investigations drastically impact lives. For witnesses, a murder investigation could put their life in danger. For the killer, an investigation means covering their tracks, weaving deception and lies, possibly running and hiding, or contemplating more murders, and if accountability prevails, spending part or most of their lives behind bars. For friends and family members of the victim, the investigation could mean prolonged grief, unwanted publicity, and stigmatization. Depending upon what information has been released, members of the community may become prejudiced for or against the victim, for or against the victim's family and friends, for or against the suspects, or for or against the suspect's family and friends. If both the victim and the murderer are members of the same family or circle of friends, an investigation could mean taking sides in the case and choosing between friends and family members with differing opinions. Murder is emotionally volatile. Tolerance for differing thoughts and opinions naturally runs thin among those directly affected.

Survivors may believe it is safer and more appropriate for law enforcement and investigative personnel with more training and objectivity to initiate the investigation. Some survivors are silenced by fear of retaliation by the murderer(s). Some survivors fear being perceived as the hostile paranoid leader of a bereaved posse obsessed with revenge for their losses. Other survivors are reluctant for fear of getting others in trouble for indiscretions and illicit activities that may be peripherally related to the murder. Still others are reluctant because they fear that the wrong people might come under suspicion. In the early stages of a homicide investigation, potential motives are considered, and everyone is a suspect. Survivors often become suspects if they were in the midst of any conflicts or disputes with the victim, were the beneficiary of life insurance policies, or the heir to the victim's estate. As a survivor, it is hard not to resent the fact that you are viewed as a potential perpetrator and treated in the same way as the person who actually committed the inconceivable despicable act. Typically, the more honest you are with investigators and the more cooperative you are in providing information to police, the more quickly they will stop looking at you as a suspect. Since police believe you should have nothing to hide if you are innocent, cooperation is an unspoken expectation. Nothing to hide does not mean that your family has no skeletons or secrets. The assumption is that no secret is too grave to share in the face of murder.

Sometimes survivors wait so long to come forward, they fear their information will be regarded as stale and their motives for coming forward will be questioned. Some are reluctant simply because they are overwhelmed with shock and grief and do not have the emotional energy to contend with the possibility of murder much less the process and realizations that reporting a murder set in motion. Coming forward with a possible murder case is a big decision to make. In the early and intensive phases of grief, paying attention to anything beyond taking the next breath is a lot to expect. Intense emotionality can impair powers of observation.

Survivors may have self-doubts about their own suspicions and feel apprehensive about gambling with their credibility by being the first to come forward. Many fear they will not be believed. Many survivors do not feel qualified or confident enough to point a finger and say "murder." Survivors may ask themselves, "Who am I to second-guess the police? They were at the scene of death. Of course, if there were reason to suspect murder, the police would be all over this case." Survivors may hold back their suspicions waiting for more compelling evidence to emerge to make them more credible in the eyes of authorities when they do come forward. Survivors may believe the police are on the job covertly investigating the death. "If I can detect foul play they must too."

Joining the oblivious and waiting for the journey of justice to jump start itself can be tempting, but the false comforts wear thin quickly. Questions of social responsibility and honor emerge. Will your failure to come forward with pertinent concerns and information implicate you as a suspect or be construed as obstruction of justice if a serious investigation should evolve? Do the values, beliefs, and laws that you ascribe to obligate you to come forward? Are we obligated to protect others by doing all we can to hold murderers accountable? Are we obligated to turn our lives inside out and upside down to pursue a justice that may not come to fruition? Ultimately, our pursuits change nothing for our murdered loved one. Are we obligated to complicate our lives and endanger ourselves? Are we obligated to our loved one to uncover the truth they are not here to reveal, at any price?

Nobody can answer these questions for you. Your only legal obligation is to not obstruct justice and to not bear false witness (i.e., do not commit perjury). Beyond obstruction and perjury, any actions and inactions on the road to justice are at the individual survivor's discretion. Sometimes doing the right thing means holding on tightly to what is left and other times it means putting everything on the line to get justice—safety, reputation, privacy, credibility, resources, and time. Regrettably, relationships are often fractured by controversial feelings about what to risk and how to proceed.

Regardless of who first detects the murder and initiates the investigation, survivors eventually bump into the question, "What is my role in the murder case? As a survivor, how should I be regarded by the justice system? As a leader, follower, watchdog, witness, informant, knight of justice, spokesperson, or suspect?" Our justice system does not afford a specific role to survivors, which can deepen feelings of powerlessness and anxiety. The ambiguity leaves too much room for conflict and misunderstanding. Each survivor's role is informally negotiated on an individual case-by-case basis. The outcome depends upon the attitudes of prosecutors and investigators, the circumstances of the murder, trust and credibility issues between the survivor and law enforcement, how much information the survivor is independently privy to, or any variety of perceived risks or opportunities. Professionals in the system can either collaborate with survivors on some level and help give shape to their role, or attempt to exclude the survivor from the process altogether. Survivors need to be prepared to advocate for their role in the murder case.

Before anything, survivors need to consider for themselves how involved they want to be? How involved can they be? The time and energy involved in following your loved one's murder case is incredibly demanding. Depending upon the nature of your involvement, your activities might include meeting with investigators from various levels of law enforcement, meeting with the prosecutors, meeting with the medical examiner, communicating with judges and probation departments, attending preparatory meetings for court proceedings, meeting and possibly retaining attorneys for independent legal advice, filing civil suits against the murderer, retaining private investigators, attending pretrial hearings, attending the trial, attending the sentencing hearing, attending appeals hearings and retrials, attending parole board meetings, and more. Survivors often scratch their heads years after their loved one's murder and say, "My God, for the past three years this murder case has consumed every sick, vacation, and personal leave day, and every extra dollar I own, and we still do not have accountability." Working on behalf of the murder victim can cost survivors relationships and opportunities. Life can quickly evolve into a maze revolving around the murder, the murder victim, and consequentially, around the murderer. At times, the pursuit of justice can feel like an anchor to hell.

At first, many survivors believe their only role and responsibility is to go to the authorities and tell them everything they know about their loved one's death, and then leave it to the police to investigate the case, provide some answers, and apprehend the murderer. For some survivors, this is how the road to justice goes. But far too many survivors discover that simply sharing their concerns with police and asking them to please "look into it" are not enough. Getting a proper investigation is not always easy, especially if the police have already made up their mind about the case and consider it closed or unsolvable. One of the biggest roadblocks to justice is officials who are professional, polite, pretend to be concerned and responsive, but ultimately do nothing. A proper investigation is something that has to be persistently fought for, demanded, and sometimes even purchased through the use of private investigators, labs, and lawyers.

The murder is the first betrayal and for too many survivors, the attitude and failures of law enforcement and the justice system are the other betrayals. The process of justice essentially demands that survivors surrender control of their loved one's murder case to a stranger at the very time they are still trying to comprehend the reality that someone, possibly someone close to them, committed the ultimate betrayal against them and their loved one.

Survivors quickly discover that the real road to justice is not jam-packed with action and suspense like the valiant sagas we see on television. The path to justice is paved with bureaucracy and littered with potholes pooled deep with ineptitude, indifference, corruption, and laws that flap in the face of public safety. We are repeatedly fooled by elusive mirages of justice and left wondering which if any of them are real. Hope for justice can start waxing and waning early in the investigative process. Survivors often endure phases when hope trickles completely dry. We stand lost and listless in the desert of justice thirsty and praying for rain. The momentum of an investigation can be weak and prolonged or seemingly nonexistent. The road to justice winds in circles as investigative updates to the survivor repeat old information as if it were fresh. The updates become less frequent, and it becomes harder to get anyone to return a phone call. The unsatisfied consumer of justice is often perceived as a source of chronic irritation and a sore reminder of failure, hopelessness, and helplessness.

Do not be intimidated. Do not accept indifference and inaction. Collecting the evidence to confirm or disconfirm the possibility of murder is something we as taxpayers pay our law enforcement officials to do. Requesting an investigation is really nothing more than asking our publicly paid professionals to do something that they have already been paid to do. Professionals who deal with death, are by routine, supposed to ask the question, "Could this be murder?" about any unnatural death. Remind yourself that there are no qualifications necessary to ask the question, "Could this be murder?" The question is legitimate.

You do not have to build the case for police before coming forward with your concerns. All investigations begin with questions.

Even if further investigation proves your suspicions unfounded, there is absolutely nothing wrong with insisting on a proper investigation so that everyone can know instead of speculate. If a professional who deals with crime cannot take the death of another human being seriously enough to do their job thoroughly, they should be helped into other careers where they do not pose a threat to public safety.

Sometimes investigations are covert and pounce swiftly like a cat on a mouse when the time is right and the evidence is ripe. Other times, the case is overtaken by inertia. From the survivor's perspective, it can be very hard to tell what is *really* going on with the case. Investigators make unofficial decisions regarding how much effort and resources to devote to a case. Even though the case is officially open, they may stop investing time and resources into solving the crime.

As long as the case is open, investigators can withhold information from survivors by arguing that it is an open case and they are obliged to protect the integrity of the evidence. In denying access to evidence and information, the police are essentially hindering survivors from pursuing the investigation independently. Police sometimes use the open status of a case to cover their own failures. They may feel threatened by people who want to solve the case they did not solve. They might fear the process will uncover a shoddy initial investigation. Cases are closed or abandoned for numerous reasons. If the case is closed, technically all the evidence, reports, and findings become public information giving survivors and private investigators more information for their work. If the case is closed, you will want to ask police and prosecutors to share their findings, reports, and conclusions with you. You will also want to explain why you believe an investigation is still warranted. Your concerns and information may be enough to reopen the case.

Survivors often report feeling that authorities received their concerns and information with an aura of skepticism, devil's advocacy, professional condescension, indifference, insensitivity, suspicion, or worst of all pretension. Survivors frequently leave their first contact with police in disbelief and confusion regarding the underlying meaning of the reaction they received. "Is this how officers are trained to act?" "I hope he's really going to look into it, he didn't sound particularly interested." "He didn't ask many questions." "She cut me off before I could finish telling her everything I needed to share." "Is this the officer's way of communicating objectivity and control?" "The investigator seemed more interested in his questions than my answers." "I didn't feel heard or taken seriously." "I think the detective was trying to provoke me by making subtle accusations." These reactions are a reflection on the police, not you. If you encounter discouraging attitudes, be careful not to internalize them. They will only drain the energy and confidence you need to advocate for justice in your loved one's name.

Whenever plausible, bring someone with you when you meet with police. One, you may react emotionally to the encounter, and it helps to have someone there who can step in on the conversation as needed if you need a moment to collect your thoughts and emotions. Two sets of ears work better than one. Survivors are often in a state of shock and grief that hinders observation and comprehension skills. Psychologically, there is strength in numbers. It is harder for an investigator to pull off an indifferent attitude when there are two people or more to answer to. You may also need someone there to validate you afterward by saying, "You did the right thing." You may want to consider the demeanor and disposition of the person you choose to accompany you. If you are volatile, you may want to bring a friend who is diplomatic, good at calming people, and re-establishing constructive communication. If you tend to be soft spoken or easily intimidated by authority, you may want to bring a friend who is confident and outspoken.

There is a lot survivors need to learn rapidly to advocate for justice effectively. Survivors need to understand their rights and the criminal's rights. They need to understand the general process of justice all the way from the murder, through the investigation, through the prosecution, through the trial, to conviction, sentencing, incarceration, appeals, and parole hearings. Survivors need to become aware of their options and available resources so they can advocate effectively. Survivors are expected to evolve rapidly under extreme duress to serve a cause thrust upon them under the gravest of circumstances.

Many survivors go through a very necessary and important period of obsession with the case and urgent learning following their loved one's murder. Survivors often find their role is keeping investigators true to their obligations by asking for accountability and watching to see if accountability is delivered. To assume this role effectively, survivors need to have knowledge of the laws and protocols that pertain to the investigation and prosecution of the case. Survivors may need to gain an understanding of the forensic and investigative standards, techniques, and findings. State of the art technology exists but is not necessarily sought and employed by investigators without prompting, especially if the test is costly. You cannot ask if a specific forensic test has been performed if you do not know the test exists. If you are going to "push" someone to do their job, it helps to know something about the procedures and protocols to which they subscribe. Survivors may need to develop skills in communication, public relations, and politics in order to effectively use all the resources available to the pursuit of justice. With a learning curve like this, obsession may be the survivor's most valuable asset.

Although survivors are not given a clear role in the investigation, their involvement can seriously impact the murder case in both positive and negative ways. Survivors need to be cognizant of how their words and behaviors can influence the case.

The desire to seek out those with knowledge about your loved one's death is normal. Be mindful that these people are also potential witnesses in the murder case. Ideally, survivors should avoid the role of interviewing witnesses about the murder, especially when initiating contact with individuals they would not associate with normally. Contacting and interviewing witnesses could be construed as tampering with evidence. You do not want the testimony of witnesses to be discredited by accusations that you biased them, conspired with them, or shared information about the murder case with them that they would not otherwise have known. The situation becomes particularly awkward if the potential witness is a friend or family member with whom, under normal circumstances, the survivor might choose to talk with at length about their loved one's murder.

Survivors need to assess the risks of talking about the case and establish their boundaries accordingly on an individual by individual basis. Even among trusted friends, survivors are often left with the lurking anxiety that they said too much or said the wrong thing to the wrong person.

Interacting with potential witnesses can be doubly awkward if the police have not interviewed them yet. There are people who will choose to come to survivors with information before going to police. They may tell survivors what they know to seek a sense of affirmation or guidance about what needs to be done. They may share information with survivors out of a sense of respect for the emotional reactions the survivor might have to the information and the need to have that reaction as privately as possible. The legally safest role survivors can assume is that of a pointer—pointing potential witnesses to investigators and pointing investigators to potential witnesses.

Survivors need to be mindful about interfering with the chain of evidence. When a survivor touches a piece of evidence, its integrity and admissibility in court are immediately brought into question. Remember, no matter what you do, no matter how much integrity you have, you are perceived as a biased party in your loved one's murder case. Police are reluctant to accept evidence that they did not collect themselves, yet survivors may be more likely than police to stumble upon pertinent evidence, especially if the police overlooked the evidence or if the crime scene was not properly secured. Survivors often possess or have access to their loved one's belongings, vehicles, and homes. In some instances the crime scene may even be the survivor's home. Reasonable expectations would predict that the victim's survivors, biased or not, could run across valuable evidence.

As a survivor praying for that piece of evidence to emerge that will lock-in justice, the first impulse may be to push the process hard, collect the evidence yourself, dump it on the investigator's desk and say, "Here's the evidence, now go arrest a murderer." Rules regarding discovery and collection of evidence can gravely impact the usefulness of evidence and testimony in court. Despite the urge to expedite the investigation, again, the safest role for the survivor is that of a persistent pointer—pointing investigators to evidence.

If you run across potential evidence, observe the evidence, but avoid touching or moving it if possible. Contact investigators and ask that they respond to the scene to examine and collect the newfound evidence. Photographing and/or photocopying evidence is never a bad idea. You may need proof that the evidence existed in the event it is lost or stolen from police storage. Request copies and/or receipts for anything you submit as evidence. There are instances when photos taken by laymen are admitted as evidence in court. You may also want to keep a dated journal and document all findings you turn over to police. Written correspondence to police summarizing potential evidence and leads can become valuable documentation later, if needed, to help pressure investigators into action on the case. Even if police cannot share their findings with you, they should be able to commit to looking into a lead or informing you that they are not pursuing it so you can privately follow-up on the lead if you so choose. Serving as an investigative pointer can become exasperating when leads seem to be ignored, potential witnesses are not interviewed, critical forensic tests are not run, or physical evidence is not collected. Survivors often have to be very persistent in their pointing to get a proper investigation.

Every survivor fears running out of people to talk to about their loved one's murder before they find someone who cares about how their loved one died *and* is in a position to do something about it. Many, many survivors reach a point of bleakness, especially in situations that present extraordinary challenges to law and justice such as cases where the victim's body has been destroyed or has not been found, cases with no witnesses, well-staged accidents and suicides, cases involving organized crime, or cases involving negligence, cover-up, and corruption.

Getting the right people in the law and justice system to listen entails getting many people talking. Floods of mail, phone calls, and emails have a way of getting someone's attention very quickly. There are many people out there, especially among the ranks of fellow murder victim survivors and supporters, who can be called upon as allies in advocating for a proper investigation. There are resources listed in the appendix of this book that can help you find individuals and organizations which advocate for a thorough investigation. Do not be afraid to seek out support when you need it. There is strength in numbers.

The most valuable asset you have as a survivor is your right to free speech—if you use it wisely. You have the right to speak about issues pertinent to your loved one's case to whomever you can get to listen. The key to advocating for justice is getting the right people to listen. The right people may be the commissioner of police, state and federal regulatory and advisory officers, governors, states attorneys, congressmen, victims' advocacy groups, the media, or fellow community members.

You need to bring your loved one's case to those with the power and resources to launch a serious investigation. If you are not satisfied that the investigators are taking your concerns seriously, if pertinent points have not been investigated, or key findings have not made it from the police to the prosecutor, you may want to consider going directly to the district attorney or state attorney's office. The district attorney or state's attorney is in a better position to elicit a response from law enforcement than you are. Generally, cases become known to prosecutors when a warrant for arrest is requested. Ideally, the prosecutors work with police or use their own investigative staff to get all the information they need to prosecute the case. Unfortunately, sometimes pertinent points get lost in the communication between police and prosecutors, especially in jurisdictions where the police-prosecutor relationship is ill-defined. If you are unsuccessful in prompting action locally, you may want to contact law enforcement agencies at different levels such as the state police, or possibly a federal agency such as the FBI, DEA, CIA, or ATF. Cases do not always fit under their jurisdictional definitions, but sometimes all it takes is an inquiry by another agency to get the case moving.

You can push for a proper investigation by bringing your loved one's case to the public. The media can be an effective means of raising public interest in your loved one's case. Publicity helps because it brings others into the fold so that you are no longer the only one demanding an investigation. However, the media has the potential to do as much harm as good. Survivors need to understand that anything they say to the media can significantly impact the case, especially prior to the arrest or trial. Even indicating there is a homicide investigation at all is sometimes too much information. Media coverage can tip off the murderer causing them to be more cautious and consequently hindering police from gathering more incriminating evidence. If information gets leaked to the media that previously only a few persons involved with the murder knew, the information loses authenticity in the courtroom. The defense may ask a witness, "Do you know this because you witnessed it, or did you read it in the newspaper?" No matter how the witness answers, their credibility in testimony has been weakened. Media coverage can also make it hard to find a jury that has not already been introduced to the case by the newspapers. The trial may need to be tried in another venue to get an unbiased jury.

The media can slant and twist people's words, creating misunderstandings and conflict. It can be extremely helpful to discuss with the police, prosecutors, and victims advocates, the issue of what should and should not be shared with the media. Such conversations help survivors decide how to handle the media and what they can expect to read and see in the news. Leaks from within the system and without sometimes occur and are often followed by a period of finger-pointing. Some survivors have had the unpleasant experience of being made into a scapegoat by police who cannot honor a gag order. Misinformation in the media may also be used as an instrument to test witnesses' credibility and accountability. If it is purposely reported incorrectly, the authenticity of potential witnesses can more readily be determined. The media is a wild card. The outcome of playing this card can be unpredictable, but it is a card you never want to discard. There may come a time in the investigation when media coverage becomes a valuable tool in breathing new life into the murder case. The longer a case goes unsolved or un-prosecuted, the less there is to lose by coming forward and publicly advocating for justice.

Survivors may also consider contacting investigative reporters or individuals and organizations that advocate for victims and try to promote safety, justice, and case closure as well, such as Parents of Murdered Children, Citizens for Case Closure, Crime Stoppers, America's Most Wanted (see Appendix A). These organizations have connections and resources that they can lend to your cause.

Many districts have victims' advocates that inform survivors of their rights, update them on the progress of the case, serve as liaison with law enforcement officers and prosecutors, help educate survivors on the criminal justice process, and accompany them as needed to court proceedings. Survivors have mixed experiences with victims' advocates. Some are never contacted by the victims' advocate or contacted so late in the process that it hardly makes any difference. Other survivors experience victims' advocates as a hired wall to insulate investigators and prosecutors from survivors. Others find victims' advocates extremely supportive but essentially as powerless as the survivor in the larger scheme.

With or without the blessings of "the system" and the "authorities that be," survivors can do a lot to find justice in their loved one's name. Some aspects of the survivors' roles are becoming more clearly defined by victims' rights legislation and advocacy, but they vary from state to state. Some examples of these rights are:

— Right to be notified, attend court proceedings, bail hearings, and parole hearings.
— Right to compensation and restitution for damages and counseling services.
— Right to freedom from intimidation and harassment by the defendant.
— Right to present input at various stages of the criminal justice process such as plea bargaining, pretrial release, sentencing, and parole.
— Right to be informed of the release or escape of the perpetrator.
— Right to have victim's property returned to survivors.
— Right to be notified of all the victim rights legislation.

Although these rights can vary considerably from state to state and may not ensure justice, they do help ensure survivor involvement in their loved one's case.

If you feel yourself growing sour on the whole process of justice, it is important to distinguish your frustration with the system from your frustration with the individuals working in the system. If you are prejudiced by your anger and generalize it too much, you run the risk of alienating individuals who can help you. Despite the failures of justice, there are individuals in the law enforcement and justice system who devote every working day to making up for the shortcomings of the system. These dedicated people are the ones to seek as you pick your way through the criminal justice system. They may or may not be people who are in positions of power, but they can make a difference simply because they are familiar with how the system works. Look for the people who have hearts, values, a helping spirit, and a passion for justice. Your ability to make the distinction between the flaws of the system versus the flaws of the individuals working in the system depends upon your ability to understand how the system typically works. Understanding how the system works and following your loved one's case through that system will depend upon your ability to forge alliances with those who know how to navigate the justice system and who will keep you informed about the handling of the case.

Many survivors are driven to work on the case to the point that they feel guilty for the attention it takes away from their family and other significant relationships. The case tugs and tugs on the mind and spirit preventing the survivor from being wholly present with any other activity. Although the drive to devote every waking moment to figuring out the case, finding the truth, proving the truth, and seeing that justice is done is pretty normal, it is not necessarily healthy. Survivors need to find ways to balance their priorities. Picture the murder case as a coat that you can hang up or take down. Make sure you give yourself adequate time to put on the coat and devote 100 percent of your attention to the case. Additionally, give yourself at least some time every day to take the coat off, attend to, and think about other aspects of your life. If you notice your mind wandering to murder, simply say "later" and return your thoughts to other things. Remind yourself that stepping away from the mental trenches of murder for awhile can provide a fresh perspective and re-energize you. Picking up and putting down the case is excellent mental training that will help you come into balance. Balance will stop you from letting the case lead you to neglect other aspects of your life so badly that your well-being and the well-being of your family are jeopardized.

Staying informed and involved in a murder case is hard emotional and mental work. If you do not allow time to recoup, the murder will suck the lifeblood out of you. You will be trudging on until there is nothing left of you, and you can go no further.

Exhaustive efforts may be a way to honor the deceased, but they are a sure course to dishonor the living. Remind yourself to come up for air and live a little in between grieving and working on the case. You will actually be more effective in the long run.

The road to justice is a journey that tests the endurance of your faith and spirit, and measures your willingness to make sacrifice after sacrifice in the name of justice and in the name of your loved one. There is plenty to sacrifice without giving up total quality of life to the murder case. The murderer destroyed one life, do not allow them to destroy the quality of the lives of everyone that loved the victim. Commitment to justice in your loved one's name can be balanced with quality of life. You can devote yourself to justice without losing yourself to murder.

When the investigation produces enough evidence to prove who murdered your loved one, the case is moved into the prosecuting phase. The wheels of justice can churn slowly between the investigating phase and the prosecuting phase. In my brother's case, nearly two years transpired between the murder and the trial. The famous Moxley case took more than 25 years to investigate and prosecute. Perseverence is the precursor to justice, and it hinges on personal preservation, cooperation, and coordination of efforts. Sadly, many cases never make it to the prosecution phase. When the case does not go "your way," learning to balance other aspects of your life with your dedication to finding justice may be all that keeps you sane.

CHAPTER THIRTEEN

The Road To Justice: Prosecuting A Murderer

Years can pass before an investigation culminates in an arrest. Usually the police make the arrest and send their reports to the prosecutor's office (i.e., district attorney, state's attorney, or U.S. attorney). Prosecutors are government-paid attorneys responsible for bringing criminal cases from the investigation stage to either a verdict or a guilty plea. The rules and processes of prosecuting a criminal vary from state to state and even from city to city. Generally, the prosecutor reviews the evidence, the circumstances, and the criminal history of the accused and decides what charges should be filed. Prosecutors may also order additional investigation. Many prosecutors have investigative personnel who work solely for the district attorney's office. Prosecutors have great leverage in how they charge a person being accused of taking the life of another. They can go soft or hard on the accused, with charges ranging from manslaughter to capital murder, carrying sentences ranging from probation to death. Charges are subject to change as prosecutors collect more information about the murder. Charges may start high only to be played like cards in plea bargain and immunity negotiations between the prosecutor and the defense.

Most district attorneys are elected officials. They represent the people and are expected to carry out their job with the interests of the community and their constituency at heart. The selection of charges can become a highly volatile, political issue. For example, domestic abusers who murder their spouses might be dealt with more seriously in a region with well-funded, well-organized domestic violence advocacy groups or human service organizations focused on helping woman out of domestic violence situations. Murder by gun might be dealt with more seriously than other methods of murder in a state that politically discourages gun ownership with harsh gun laws. Political and cultural factors introduce variances in how similar murders are treated in different geographic and demographic settings. Standards and norms for investigating and prosecuting murders can vary drastically.

Survivors of murder victims can use political pressure and public pressure to encourage prosecutors and investigators to hold murderers fully accountable. This option may become essential if the police are failing to investigate, if the prosecutor is not taking steps to prosecute the case, or if the prosecutor's charges do not reflect the seriousness of the crime. There is nothing wrong with publicly saying that you fully expect your government officials to build the strongest case possible against the person who murdered your loved one. Exercising political and media options requires a certain degree of political savvy and also the ability to discuss your loved one's case in a way that elicits public sentiment and interest. Grief and anger do not naturally lend themselves well to public relations exercises. It is hard to maintain composure when you are threadbare with grief and anguish. Some survivors choose to hire an attorney to represent the victim's family and deflect the public glare.

The task of politically pushing justice is daunting and exhausting. Breaking down the process into simple action steps can make the job more surmountable. Step one: determine your goals. Step two: draft a letter advocating for your goals. Step three: collect the addresses of politicians, prospective supporters, and select media contacts. Public safety is an issue that should be close to the heart of all our public servants working within the justice system. Step four: mail letters. Step five: make others aware of your situation so they can write letters on your behalf as well. You would be amazed at how much impact you can have with only a mailing list and a really strong letter expressing your concerns regarding the handling of your loved one's case. There are many support and advocacy organizations that survivors can call upon for information, support, and advocacy in the political and legal arenas. A list of some of these resources is included in Appendix A.

After arrest, the prosecutor takes the murder case before the grand jury and presents them with a bill of charges against the accused murderer and introduces a summary of the evidence. The grand jury decides if there is adequate evidence to support the charges and proceed with a criminal trial. Grand juries generally consist of 15 to 23 jurors and a unanimous decision *is not* required to indict. The grand jury proceedings occur behind closed doors. The only people in attendance other than the grand jurors are the prosecutor and the selected witnesses who are present only for their testimony. The defendant does not appear before the grand jury. The defendant can, however, get transcripts of all grand jury proceedings. Prosecutors often hold back on the amount of evidence and witnesses they present to the grand jury to avoid early disclosures to the defense.

A decision to indict (i.e., a decision to formally charge and try the defendant) is known as a "true bill," and a decision *not* to indict is known as a "no bill." If the grand jury delivers a no bill, the prosecutor is allowed the opportunity to present more evidence. Grand juries have the power to recommend that the charges be modified as well. In some instances, prosecutors can bypass the grand jury process by filing a criminal complaint and presenting the evidence at a hearing before a judge. The prosecutor must convince the judge that the evidence is adequate to convict the murderer.

If the grand jury indicts the defendant, the accused is then arraigned before a judge where issues of legal representation, bail, and conditions of pretrial release may be decided. The judge can either set bail or deny bail. Bail is like a deposit that the defendant makes to the courts. The deposit is returned after the defendant appears for trial. Bail discourages defendants from fleeing before being tried. Bail also allows the accused to enjoy the freedoms of the innocent until they are proven guilty. When dealing with murderers, even the prospect of their temporary freedom is enraging and unnerving to survivors. Yet, if any one of us were accused, we would want to be treated as innocent until our guilt was proven. Judges sometimes exercise preventive detention by setting bail so high that release is not a viable option for the accused. Judges also can deny bail if the defendant is considered a public safety threat.

The defendant may plead guilty any time after the arraignment and formalize plea bargains with the prosecutor. In some states, survivors have the right to be informed about plea bargains and have input. In other states, survivor input is not guaranteed, but not prohibited by law. Defense attorneys sometimes fight vehemently against survivor input and participation in plea bargaining. If survivors want to be heard, they need to voice their position loudly and clearly to prosecutors and judges either directly and/or in writing. If nobody will listen, let prosecutors know that if they are not willing to hear you and consider what you are saying, you will reserve the right to go to those who will listen, such as the media, victim's rights advocacy organizations, mayors, governors, congressmen, state representatives, etc. If you are ignored, come back knocking on the door in numbers.

There are many survivor groups and organizations with writing campaign lists ready to go. Many people after learning about the nature of a murder and its handling will feel compelled to speak out if you give them a name, an address and a summary of the facts. The best way for a survivor to develop a network of people willing to rally for justice is to be there to rally for other survivors when they need letters to judges urging strict sentencing or letters to parole boards asking that a murderer remain incarcerated. Also, family, friends, and co-workers can ask more people to write letters.

If you exercise your right to provide input regarding plea bargaining, you need to be aware of the emotional risks you are taking. For example, if you insist that the murderer be tried instead of offered a plea bargain, you need to consider the possibility of either verdict. If the murderer is found not guilty and set free, will you blame and punish yourself for that outcome? You need to make a reasoned choice and agree not to beat up yourself because you could not foresee what the outcome of a trial would

be. There is no way to predict a verdict. There are strong cases that lose, weak cases that win, and everything in between. Sometimes the truth shines through to the jury and sometimes truth does not prevail. With or without survivor input, decisions regarding plea bargaining are ultimately made at the discretion of the prosecutor. Some states have rules and guidelines that set the parameters for plea bargaining, while others allow the prosecutor a wide girth of discretion.

Prosecutors consider many factors in addition to the input of victims and survivors. Prosecutors may plea bargain for cost and efficiency purposes. Courts are overbooked, prisons are overcrowded, and trials are expensive and require manpower that may already be spread too thin. A prosecutor also may choose to plea bargain if he or she is not confident that the case is strong enough to get a conviction. In some instances, softer charges may be traded for the defendant's cooperation in investigating and prosecuting other crimes. If the plea arrangement leads to the apprehension of someone more dangerous, then perhaps the deal is worthwhile. But in too many instances, murder charges are reduced in exchange for information leading to the apprehension of someone less dangerous, like a drug dealer with no history of violent crime.

The defendant also has many incentives to plea bargain. One, plea bargaining provides a known outcome that is agreed upon. Two, pleading guilty is viewed as a cooperative act and is generally rewarded with fewer or lighter charges. Three, plea bargains can save attorney fees, as well as eliminate all the time, energy, publicity and re-victimization involved with a trial. Plea bargaining is often the quickest, quietest, and most cost-effective way of disposing of a criminal matter.

Arraignments are generally followed by a series of pretrial or status hearings. Some of these hearings are devoted to discovery (i.e., exchanging information between prosecution and defense), mini-trials regarding the admission and exclusion of evidence, and entertaining other motions by the defense, such as entering an insanity plea or guilty plea. Other pre-trial hearings are devoted to more mundane matters such as assessing readiness for trial, adding or changing of defense attorneys and prosecutors, setting of trial dates, and postponing trial dates. Many survivors ask, "Do I really need to attend all those hearings? Sometimes they only last a few minutes, and often they are scheduled and cancelled without notification." Attendance at pre-trial proceedings is entirely up to the individual survivor. Many survivors live far away from where the case is being prosecuted and cannot feasibly attend all the court proceedings. Other survivors choose not to attend in protest to the murder case eating up even more of their energy. Pre-trial hearings can rapidly consume work time, vacation time, sick time, and family time. On the other hand, attending pretrial hearings is the best way to stay informed firsthand and make your presence and interest in the case known. Some survivors work together to make sure at least one or two people are at these hearings to represent their loved one and follow the case. I do not recommend attending court proceedings alone. The pretrial hearing is often the first face-to-face contact with the murderer since the murder or the arrest. It can be a very emotionally intense experience.

If you are planning to attend the trial, attending a pre-trial hearing is a good opportunity to familiarize yourself with the court-room atmosphere, get a feel for the judge who will be presiding over the case, and prepare yourself to tolerate the accused murderer's presence. The pre-trial experience will help you work through your emotional reactions to seeing the murderer well in advance of the trial. The initial exposure offers an opportunity to test your composure and gauge what level of emotional resilience you will need to make it through the trial. Just seeing the mur-derer for the first time can be emotionally overwhelming. I experi-enced rage pounding in my head, fire shooting from my eyes, double thumb signals pointing straight down to hell, and sarcastic venom whispering from my lips, "Oh my, I think he looks good in shackles. Don't you?" Luckily, this first reaction was not in the presence of a jury and was subtle enough that the judge, bailiffs, and defense attorneys did not notice. Body language can be enough to get survivors barred from the courtroom. With or without the right to be notified and attend court proceedings, the judge can dismiss anyone from their courtroom who is disrupting or nega-tively influencing the court proceedings. Survivors have been barred from courtrooms for crying, facial expressions, staring, speaking out to defendants, or any myriad of expressive or demonstrative acts.

To some degree the justice system wants survivors and vic-tims to remain invisible to the process. Survivors and victims are often treated like contaminated evidence by the courts because of their intense emotional involvement with the case. Survivors and victims can have a tremendous emotional impact on jurors, the media, investigators, the public, and potential witnesses, or others simply by virtue of the intense grief they bear. Deeply felt and sincere emotions are gripping to experience or witness. Second-hand grief strikes anybody with an ounce of compassion who knows or can imagine what it might be like to lose someone dear to them in a horrible way. Contact with survivors makes the victim *real*, makes the murder *real*, and can evoke powerful emotions in reaction to the murder case. For some reason, our justice system does not distinguish compassion from prejudice. Our justice system functions as if normal human compassion and outrage were the kryptonite of justice instead of embracing these qualities as the true fuel of justice. Defense attorneys grab up this kryptonite and use the emotionality triggered by the bare reality of murder to defend the murderer. "Your honor, I move for a mistrial. The jury was emotionally biased by pictures of the victim that the family wore as pins." The perception of normal human emotions by the courts can feel so very backwards.

The process of anticipating a trial, preparing emotionally, and then having it repeatedly postponed traps many survivors in a suspended state of grief and a perpetual cycle of anxiety and crisis. There are many thoughts survivors may obsess over in the weeks leading to the trial. "Am I ready to hear all that I might hear in the courtroom?" "Is the case strong enough to get a conviction?" "Can I handle a 'not guilty' verdict?" "How viciously is the defense going to attack my loved one's character?" "Will the defense try to insinuate the victim had an active role in their own demise?" "How viciously or maliciously will witnesses be cross examined?" Although survivors try to prepare themselves emotionally for the trial, there are too many unknowns to prepare for every scenario. No matter how long you have waited for the case to go to trial, there is no way to feel truly prepared for the reality and intensity of the event.

Survivors who choose to attend the trial are there because they are desperate to hear the truth, desperate for justice, desperate for accountability, or desperate to have their loved one represented in the courtroom. Desperation is not the same as emotional readiness. Ready or not, the trial will still begin. You will need tissues. You will need to ask the prosecutor if the courthouse has any private rooms for survivors to retreat to if necessary. You will want a pen and paper to take notes, if you so desire. Although rules regarding reading material in the court can vary, you may want a book to read for distraction during breaks. You will want a good cushion to sit on. The seats are usually hard, and trials can be quite lengthy. Trials have many types of breaks or interruptions that prolong the process, such as court calendars, side bars, deliberations, motions, etc.

The court calendar will not mention your loved one's name. The docket will say "The People versus Joe Murderer." There are people who will be uncomfortable and even angry with your presence such as defense attorneys, the accused murderer, or the defendant's family who generally are allotted the same seating areas as the victim's survivors. Keep in mind, to the accused murderer's family, this trial is about their loved one whose future is hanging in the balance, not about justice in your loved one's name. Survivors may be struck by a hostile undercurrent that says "you don't belong here." The perpetrator's family may believe you to be the villain and their kin to be the victim.

Sometimes the villainization is blatant and cruel. If you are accosted by angry supporters of the defendant, be peaceful, break eye contact, shake your head and walk away. Go find a seat and pull out that book I recommended that you bring or go find someone to stand near whose presence might diffuse the hostility, such as a prosecutor, a bailiff, or a judge. If you are feeling threatened or harassed, tell someone. Do not be intimidated. You are where you are supposed to be. Distinguish yourself in the courtroom through your respect for the court, tolerance, and good behavior. Regardless of how the justice system frames it up, the trial is as much about your loved one as it is about the murderer. If anybody has a right to be there, you do.

Understanding at least a little about the trial process can help dispel anxiety. The first step in a trial is jury selection. Potential jurors are asked questions that have been formulated by the defense, the prosecution, and the judge. Both the prosecution and the defense are allowed to select and reject a certain number of jurors. After jury selection, the prosecution and/or defense may make motions to introduce or exclude various pieces of evidence before the trial proceeds any further.

The prosecution and then the defense deliver opening statements which summarize and highlight the case that each side intends to prove. Jury selection and opening statements cannot be observed by prospective witnesses. The prosecution begins unfolding their case through the direct examination of witnesses. The defense then has the opportunity to cross-examine the prosecution's witnesses. Next, the prosecution is given an opportunity to re-examine the witness. The prosecution then rests. At this point the defense may make a motion to dismiss the charges as an attempt to imply to jurors that the prosecution was weak. The motion is usually denied. The defense proceeds to call and examine their witnesses following the same process except it will be the prosecution doing the cross-examining. The defense rests, and the prosecution is given opportunity to rebutt the defense's case. The judge, in consultation with the prosecution and defense, then finalizes instructions that he or she gives to the jury. The prosecution and the defense make closing arguments.

The judge instructs the jury on how to apply the law to the case. The jury then deliberates. Throughout deliberations, the jury may call the court into session to ask the judge questions which may have arisen in their deliberations, to rehear testimony read back to them by the stenographer, and to request clarification on the law. In almost all states, a unanimous vote is required to reach a verdict. Once a verdict is reached, all parties are called back into the courtroom. After the verdict is announced, the verdict is confirmed individually by every juror. The defense may make post-trial motions such as asking the judge to override the verdict and acquit the defendant, calling for a new trial, giving notice of intent to appeal, or calling for a mistrial. Only rarely are such post-trial motions granted. Sentencing is generally scheduled to take place in a separate hearing after a pre-sentencing investigation has been conducted on the murderer.

Survivors can also prepare themselves for the trial by seeking to understand some of the rights our justice system affords the criminal before actually witnessing these rights in action. As the criminal's rights are exercised, a dichotomy emerges between how defendants are treated and how victims and witnesses are treated. Seemingly well-founded rights afforded criminals are sometimes ruthlessly applied to escape accountability. For example, more emphasis is placed on how evidence is gathered than what the evidence concludes. To the observer of the process, seemingly trivial details are argued while the most critical points fade into the background of the proceedings.

The accused murderer has the right to remain silent (Fifth Amendment to the U.S. Constitution). There is no bigger obstacle to truth and justice than silence. The accused murderer does not have to take the stand, does not have to speak to their guilt or innocence, does not have to speak to their credibility, does not have to subject themselves to any questioning or public scrutiny. All they have to do is sit there and whisper in their attorney's ear every time they do not like something that was said. In fact, conferring is encouraged between the defense attorney and defendant, while private discussions among witnesses, survivors, and attorneys are frowned upon. Victims, survivors, and witnesses do not have anyone to whisper their protests to as they watch witness after witness get grilled on the stand. There is nobody to say "objection" on their behalf. Surely the accused murderer is the one who owes an explanation to society more than anyone else. Yet, our justice system gives them the right to slither through the whole accountability process without answering to anyone.

The accused murderer has the right to confront their witnesses (Sixth Amendment to the U.S. Constitution). This is known as the confrontation clause. Murderers can sit through the testimony of every witness before they take the stand themselves, if they should choose to testify on their own behalf. All other witnesses are sequestered from the courtroom so they cannot be influenced or prepared by the testimony of others. Why is our system set up to give murderer's opportunity to exploit the testimony of other witnesses, adapt their testimonies, or develop lies to distort the details of other witnesses' testimony? Our system allows the murderer to challenge the whole truth while other witnesses are only given opportunity to speak to the pieces of the truth they are asked about. If the murderer is going to testify on their own behalf, they should be made to testify both first and last. They should testify first so they do not have opportunity to use the truths and details of others to weave more convincing lies and alibis, and they should testify last so they have opportunity to answer to the statements of their accusers.

There are other problems with the confrontation clause. The clause excludes written or spoken statements from witnesses that cannot be present to be confronted by the defense. Essentially, anything the victim ever wrote or told anyone, no matter how pertinent to their murder, can ever be introduced in court directly by the prosecutor or through the testimony of other witnesses. All of the victim's testaments to others are legally deemed hearsay. Even if the victim knew prior to their murder what was coming, who was going to do the killing, and why—and shared this information with many people in case something bad was to happen—the survivor's accounts of the victim's tale would never be heard in a courtroom unless the accounts could be substantiated and brought in using evidence and testimony other than the victim's words. My brother had a lot to say to me in the months prior to his murder that pertained to the impersonation scheme that set up the motive for his murder. The jury never heard a word of my brother's version of events. Why are the words of a murderer held higher than the victim's in the courtroom?

The defendant is entitled to adequate legal representation. If the defendant cannot afford an attorney, the taxpayers foot the bill to defend the murderer. In some cases, the defendant is even given two publicly-paid defense attorneys to afford them the best defense. Public expenditures on defense can seem lavishly unfair to survivors, but sometimes in the long run assuring the defendant has good solid legal representation can help avoid cause for appeals and mistrials. The defendant's right to adequate representation leaves the backdoor open to appeals, mistrials, and reversals of guilty verdicts. Poor representation can serve as grounds for appeal.

The defendant also has the right not to be placed in double jeopardy (Fifth Amendment of the U.S. Constitution) meaning that if they are tried and found not guilty, they can never be tried again for the same crime even if more compelling evidence emerges later. The only exception is when a case is tried on the state level and then federal charges relating to the same crime are opened, and vice versa. Why does our system allow murderers multiple chances to be found innocent, but "the people" are allowed only one chance to prove guilt?

There are numerous legal strategies the murderer may use to defend themselves. Many survivors find themselves preparing for the trial on a rational level by trying to anticipate the murderer's defense. The most passive defense is the simple presumption of innocence. The burden of proof is on the prosecutor to convince twelve jurors beyond a reasonable doubt that the defendant is guilty. If the defendant can convince one juror that there is reasonable doubt, then the accused is guaranteed freedom. Accused murderers may defend themselves by claiming they killed the victim in self-defense. The defense may try to portray the victim as the aggressor. Since the victim is not there to defend themselves, the murderer does not encounter much resistance in establishing self-defense arguments. Some murderers try to evade criminal punishment by claiming insanity. If the accused is found to be insane, they will be committed to a mental institution instead of a prison. Insanity is very hard to establish. Accused murderers may base their defense upon establishing alibis (evidence that the accused was somewhere else at the time the murder was committed).

Our justice system does not treat witnesses very well. Prior to the trial, witnesses are commonly asked not to speak about the case. Although there is clearly a need to uphold the integrity of the case, it is painful for witnesses to keep gruesome details alive and ready to attest to for months and years. Keeping a journal of events and recollections about the murder is one approach to preserving the details you will be testifying to in the future. A journal can minimize the need to keep memories active in the conscious mind 24/7.

A word of caution about journals—they are best kept private and factual. Journals can be subpoenaed by either the defense or the prosecution as evidence, meaning you could be cross-examined on everything you write no matter how personal and subjective. Every opinion, every bias, every mood in your journal could be exploited by the defense. Powerful word associations rather than in-depth journaling are recommended. Usually people who are recalling the truth have very vivid memories when triggered. There is nothing wrong with using notes to prompt your memories. Cues can encourage consistent and accurate testimony. If you are asked in court about journals and notes, you will want to testify truthfully.

Notes may improve the validity of your testimony in the eyes of jurors. So, how do you keep a journal and testify honestly about its existence without running the risk of it being subpoenaed? Some survivors condense their original works to outlines. Outlines can be just as effective in triggering memories, but do not provide the defense with as much room to distort the meaning or intent of your private thoughts. Replacing journals with outlines is only effective if you make your journals non-subpeonable (i.e., no longer in existence). Do not worry. You can always use your outlines to recreate your journals after the trial if you are so compelled.

The silence required of witnesses prior to the trial heightens their isolation. By the time the trial comes, witnesses are often desperate to share their truth and scared to death about how they might react to that most painful truth being challenged by the murderer's hired axe whose job is to chop holes in the testimony. The urgency of truth is whetted by the oath every witness takes before taking the stand: "Tell the truth, the whole truth, and nothing but the truth." Yet, our system of criminal justice does a lousy job of listening to witnesses and allowing them to express their whole truth. Once testimony is whittled down to the admissible components that prosecutors and defense attorneys deem pertinent, the truth looks like a film editing room. Most of the truth is left lying on the cutting room floor. There is so much the jury never hears.

Witnesses often feel gagged, even in the courtroom, by all the narrow-pointed questions, questions that are not asked, objections, and perhaps even attacks on their credibility and personal character by the defense. Character attacks are often ploys to distract jurors from the content of a witness's testimony by presenting them with value judgments about the witness to grapple with instead. As a witness, it can be tempting to argue a point or snap at provocative defense attorneys, but avoid this trap at all costs. Some attorneys will try to engage the witness in argument to bring out their worst side and beleaguer their point that the defendent is being victimized. Do your best to speak your truth calmly and non-defensively. The prosecutor can give you opportunity to clarify points that the defense may have distorted during redirect. In testimony, calmness, confidence, and collectedness often translate into credibility.

Many witnesses step down from the stand feeling robbed of what they perceive as their right to fulfill the oath they just took to tell the whole truth. Very seldom does a witness step down feeling like everything they needed and wanted to say was heard. Very seldom do witnesses feel they did a good job after being cross examined. The very nature of cross examination is to confuse, discredit, and cause discomfort. Witnesses may feel like they have just been victimized again by being publicly humiliated right before the eyes of the accused murderer. There is an irony in being questioned publicly by the murderer's representative when you are not allotted the option of asking the murderer your questions.

Many survivors develop an intense dislike of defense attorneys. The defense attorney's role is to assure that proper procedure and respect for their client's rights are adhered to, but far too many defense attorneys take their role too far. Trials become solely about winning, no matter what their client did, no matter how they have to twist the truth, no matter how they tear innocent people apart to win. Whether they justify their actions as "just doing our jobs" or not, they are still accountable before themselves and before their higher power for all they hurt. Sometimes doing the right thing is costly. Sometimes doing the right thing means doing your job differently. Sometimes doing your job is holding tight to your values and letting your client face the consequences for what they did. Setting a murderer free should be no one's job. The interpretation of the premise, "it is better for a guilty man to walk free than for an innocent man to be falsely imprisoned" has become a perversion of the system. There is a distinction between freeing the innocent and setting the guilty free.

The aftermath of murder involves many competing definitions for justice. For some, justice is unveiling the truth, convicting the murderer(s), and making them serve a sentence commensurate with their crimes and violations against humanity. For others, justice is having their innocence legally proven. For others, justice is nothing more than successfully manipulating the system to evade accountability and incarceration for crimes committed.

CHAPTER FOURTEEN

The Verdict and Beyond

As much as we try, there is no way to see clearly beyond the verdict until it comes. Everything leading up to the verdict is so incredibly intense. So much weighs on "guilty" or "not guilty." In preparation for either outcome, survivors may develop some expectations about how the verdict will affect them emotionally or otherwise. When the verdict finally comes, it usually brings forth a lot of disillusionment because some of these expectations may have been unrealistic. Grief does not diminish with the conclusion of the trial, it takes on new dimensions. Survivors are often shocked to discover that even a guilty verdict does not offer real closure in regards to how the murderer will be dealt with in the criminal justice system. The trial work ends only to be replaced with other lifelong tasks such as finding a way to live with the facts of the murder, the reality of the verdict, and the enforcement of the sentencing.

The delivery of the verdict is a solemn moment that marks time. Announcement of the verdict will bring relief to some and outrage to others. The murderer is delivered freedom or accountability. The victim is delivered justice or betrayal. Everyone is waiting to learn whose definition of justice will prevail. Everyone's future is hanging in the balance. Everyone's credibility is hanging in the balance. The wait for the verdict is long and restless. Even when there is nothing more that can be done, the drive for justice continues to circle.

If you or your family members plan on making any statements to the media after the verdict, this is your last chance to prepare them. Keep in mind, your emotions will be in full gear after the verdict, and it might be difficult to compose strong cohesive statements on the spot. You will need to consider what to say or not say in the event of either verdict.

When the court is called into session to hear the verdict, time stops and everyone that believes in a higher power starts quietly and discreetly praying. The left hand holds the right and they squeeze each other nervously in anticipation. "Please God. Please God. Please God. Please God...." You may shake and feel weak and nauseous. As you wait, remind yourself that no matter what the outcome, you are not responsible for the verdict. The only thing you are responsible for at this point is conducting yourself in the most respectable manner possible.

If you believe the defendant is guilty of murder and the verdict comes back "not guilty," take a deep breath and just sit. A "not guilty" verdict delivered to a killer is every murder victim survivor's worst nightmare. All survivors try to prepare themselves emotionally for the possibility of a "bad" verdict, but you never know until the moment the verdict is delivered how you will handle it. The feelings of betrayal, defeat, and rage that come with a "bad" verdict are a force to contend with, but you do not have to contend with all of it full force right here and now. Public outbursts and hasty decisions will only make you more vulnerable and make the murderer look more calm and credible. Take another deep breath and know that the wind is still blowing, the sun is still shining, the rain is still falling, you are still breathing, people are still dying, and babies are still being born. If you do not self-destruct with negativity or blow off your own foot with explosive emotions, you will get through this gut-wrenching letdown.

Although some people may view the verdict as a reflection of credibility—the defendant's credibility, the witnesses' credibility, the investigator's credibility, the survivors' credibility—do not buy into this trapped thinking. The verdict is not always the equivalent of truth. Our justice system was designed deliberately so that a guilty man would go free before an innocent man was convicted. Consequently, guilty people sometimes go free. Unfortunately, the victims and their survivors are the sacrificial lambs of the justice system. You are suffering the pain of the injustice so that a fellow citizen might not have to endure the pain of being falsely convicted. You personally are suffering the downside of the rights all citizens enjoy. Even if the rights of the murderer were held higher than your loved one's rights, resist the temptation to feel that they were discredited or devalued. Whether it is recognized or not, you deserve a purple heart in your loved one's name to recognize the sacrifice of justice you are enduring.

The verdict does not necessarily reflect the truth. Frequently the verdict is a reflection of the preponderance of evidence, the laws, the skill and resources invested in the case, or the spin placed upon the lawyer's presentation of arguments. As survivors, you did not investigate the case, you did not try the case, and you did not cause the justice system to fail. Unfortunately, there may be absolutely nothing you can do to fix the outcome. The murderer cannot be tried again. Do not speak a word or take a single action until you understand that a bad verdict is a problem you cannot fix or compensate for by reacting impulsively. All you can do at this point is focus on what is best for you and your loved ones who are still alive.

There is a high probability that you may encounter reporters or news teams eager to record your reaction to the verdict. There may also be supporters of the murderer eager to publicly rub the verdict in your face. Although the temptation is to throw yourself on the floor and howl at the top your lungs from here to eternity, your best bet is to just stay where you are seated and take a deep breath. Then stay where you are seated and take another deep breath, and stay where you are seated. If you do not feel ready to make a statement to the media, stay seated, and remember the words "no comment." If you would like to make a statement but not at this moment, try arranging a specific date and time to render your statement after careful contemplation and preparation.

Chances are the media will follow the defendant out of the building to capture their reactions and statements. If you do not feel ready to see the defendant walk away freely with their family, stay seated. Sit for as long as you can and as long as you need. When you feel composed enough to make it from the courtroom to your car without doing or saying anything that will hurt you in the long run, then and only then should you leave. Be sure to walk with your head up. You have suffered a tremendous setback, but you have not lost the real war. The real war against violence is won in your heart, not in the courtroom.

Although the defendant cannot be tried criminally again for the same crime, you can file a civil suit against the murderer for wrongful death. In civil court, the rules are more equal-handed between the plaintiff and defendant. The defendant can be called as a witness and required to testify, whereas in criminal court they are not required to testify. In civil court, the defendant can be proven guilty by only a preponderance of the evidence (i.e., greater than half), whereas in criminal court, guilt must be proven beyond a reasonable doubt. If found guilty in a civil suit, the murderer is court-ordered to pay the plaintiff a financial settlement. The financial award is an attempt to compensate the survivors for the losses and suffering caused by the murder. The ruling is not jail time, but it is official validation of guilt. There is also satisfaction in knowing that the murderer will be reminded of what they did every time they open their paycheck and see the garnishment for years to come. Be aware, there is a statute of limitations on filing wrongful death suits. You will need to find out what the statute is in your state to make sure you do not lose the opportunity to file. If in doubt, file the suit. You can always drop the case later if you have a change of heart.

If you believed the defendant was guilty of murder, there is nothing quite as validating as hearing the word *"guilty"* repeated twelve times, once by each juror. The verdict finally lifts the question of guilt and the uncertainty of justice from your hands. You no longer have to consider yourself the murderer's number one adversary. Twelve strangers, the prosecutors, the judges, and the witnesses have joined you. After months and years of running the arguments for and against guilt through your head, you can finally let the debate fall to rest from your everyday thoughts. Having the murderer's guilt made public and knowing the murderer will not be going free anytime soon is a tremendous relief. Bask in this sense of relief for as long as you can, because in so many other ways the work has just begun.

Getting past the trial helps survivors move into new phases of healing and grief. But do not expect too much at first. Although in the long-run getting a conviction can do wonders for the survivor's healing, initially after the trial, survivors may feel like the murder just happened. Even when survivors get the trial outcome they hoped for, grief takes on new dimensions after the verdict.

The verdict often comes with a subtle or not-so-subtle pressure to celebrate, be happy, and return to normal life. Some survivors find it hard to celebrate the verdict, even if the event is worthy of being honored and recognized. The meaning of the verdict only begins to sink in at the time it is read. Many survivors find that after relief, the second reaction is disappointment accompanied by anger and profound sadness. We fought the good fight and won, but our loved one is still dead and we still feel the anguish of their loss. Some survivors string themselves along the road to justice with the subconscious fantasy that somehow if the murderer is found guilty, life as they once knew it will return. The real verdict shreds the last remnants of denial and bargaining as we realize, "The verdict may have changed everything for the murderer, but it didn't really change a thing for my loved one. Despite all the energy and resources expended, my loved one is still dead." The doors open to whole new depths of grief.

Energy that was once consumed by the battle for justice is now free to fuel the grieving process. Emotionally, grieving can be more painful than fighting for justice. Most survivors take in details of the murder at the trial that they do not begin to digest until later. At the same time, others around the survivor might believe the verdict means closure. Survivors are often in the awkward position of plummeting to new depths of grief and traumatization at the very time others are expecting them to be "over it."

After the verdict is read, a date is set for sentencing. Judges generally decide the murderer's punishment, with the exception of capital cases. Judges are not allowed to sentence someone to death unless a jury recommends it. Judges are also required to follow the sentencing laws and guidelines governing their state or jurisdiction. These guidelines set ranges in sentencing for each specific charge. The judge also may order a pre-sentencing investigation. Pre-sentencing profiles provide the judge with information about the murderer that helps determine the appropriate sentence. The judge may consider the criminal history of the murderer, the circumstances of the murder, or other pertinent pieces of information that were not presented during the trial.

The pre-sentencing profiler collects information about the convict. They may also collect impact statements from those affected by the murder and letters from members of the community expressing their concerns, opinions, and wishes regarding the murderer's punishment. At a minimum, impact statements and sentencing letters should be sent both to the probation officer doing the pre-sentencing investigation and directly to the judge that will be rendering the sentence to assure that these materials do not get overlooked. Volumes of letters and statements let the judge know that many people care and are watching for the outcome of the sentencing. Encourage friends and interested members of the community to write letters urging for maximum sentencing while the impact of the murder on the community and the individual is still fresh. These letters may help persuade the judge toward maximum sentencing, but they also are put into the murderer's file and may help persuade members of a parole board to deny release years down the line. (See sample letters in Appendix B and C.)

At the sentencing hearing, the prosecution will recommend a sentence to the judge and argue the appropriateness of that sentence. Impact statements may also be read. Most states now have laws or victims' bills of rights guaranteeing murder victim survivors the right to read an impact statement prior to sentencing. The extent to which survivors are allowed input can vary greatly from state to state and jurisdiction to jurisdiction. One court might allow only one impact statement to be read on behalf of the victim and all the survivors, while in another jurisdiction, each family member and possibly even friends are allowed to read their impact statements at the sentencing hearing.

The impact statement is the only time the victim's voice is really allowed in the courtroom, and you, the survivor, have the honor of representing them. Writing the impact statement can be both healing and painful. Oftentimes the writing of the impact statement is the first time the survivor has actually verbalized the inventory of their losses. Verbalizing the extent of your loss makes it more real. A strong impact statement should accomplish several objectives. One, make the victim real and make clear how special and irreplaceable your loved one's life was. Two, detail ways in which the victim and their survivors have suffered as a result of the murderer's actions. Losses cited can be loss of life, financial loss, loss of health, loss of well-being, loss of future, etc. Three, recommend a sentence (i.e., maximum sentence, minimum sentence, etc.).

Four, explain why the murderer is a continued threat to society.

There are different types of sentences. Indeterminate sentences offer a range of time to be served, such as 5 to 10 years, or 25 years to life. With indeterminate sentencing, after the minimum of the range has been served, survivors need to be prepared to go before the parole board to explain why maximum sentencing needs to be enforced. Many states are adopting truth in sentencing reforms which eliminate indeterminate sentencing for violent felons. Definite sentences are simpler. The prisoner is given a set number of years to serve, such as 10 years, 15 years, or life without parole.

Additionally, the judge decides whether sentences for multiple crimes, such as arson, homicide, or robbery, will be served concurrently or consecutively. If it is concurrent, the actual time served will usually be that of the longer sentence. If it is consecutive, the actual time served will be for all sentences added together. Although the judge has some leverage in what sentence gets delivered, most states have sentencing guidelines the judge must work within that lay out the parameters.

After the sentencing, survivors may want to touch base periodically with the prosecutor's office to keep informed about possible post-conviction proceedings. There are many options available to convicts to fight a guilty verdict. Many will exhaust all their options simply because they are sitting in prison with nothing to do but try, and nothing to lose by trying. In many instances, the taxpayers are footing the cost of their defense attorney, while victims and survivors in need of legal advice must use their own resources. Convicts may make motions asking the judge to declare a mistrial, which if granted, means the whole trial has to be redone. The defense will likely file for an appeal of the conviction or the sentence with the state appellate court. If the issues are not resolved at that level, the case can be appealed to the state supreme court. If the issues are not resolved at that level, the case may possibly be appealed to the U.S. Supreme Court.

In general, appellate courts overturn verdicts only if the judge made an error that could have resulted in a faulty verdict. Likewise, if the judge made legal errors in sentencing, the convict may be entitled to a new sentencing hearing. Convicts may also file for a writ of habeas corpus which essentially asks the courts to order the prisoner's release. Writs of habeas corpus are used when the convict believes they are being held in prison unlawfully or unconstitutionally. Writs of habeas corpus are generally used to address matters that cannot be addressed through the appeals process. Writs may be requested to review circumstances that were omitted from the trial proceedings, such as viable defenses that were not investigated or raised in court. Writs may be used to address rights violations that occurred in the investigation that were not heard during the trial. Motions, appeals, and writs of habeas corpus are more frequently denied than granted.

Regardless of outcome, survivors usually find the re-opening of the criminal matter re-traumatizing. Once again, they must anticipate the possibility of the murderer avoiding accountability and being set free to victimize others. Post-conviction proceedings cheat survivors from the relief they hoped they would enjoy after the conviction. Going through aspects of the justice process again and again can be frustrating, exasperating, and heartbreaking. Survivors often wonder, "Why can't we just hear all the facts, make a decision, and stick to the findings, instead of going through this hell over and over and over again. Why can't we just get it right the first time."

There are not enough incentives to get it right the first time. Lawyers and judges make a large portion of their living entertaining the hopes of convicts in a courtroom. The justice system is a vicious cycle. The convict goes after whatever hope for freedom the legal system dangles out in front of them, and the lawyers make money grasping for the convict's freedom. Our justice system is not very good at putting a stop to the cycle and saying, "Enough is enough."

After the sentencing, survivors may want to be notified in the event the murderer escapes, is released, transferred, or comes up for parole. Most states have victim registries and victim notification systems. The VINE (Victim Information and Notification Everyday) system is an example of an automated system used in many states. The victim or survivor registers and is given a personal identification number they can use to check on the convicted murderer's whereabouts and retrieve additional information should the system call to notify them of a release.

Unfortunately even victim notification systems have their

flaws. For example, when murderers are in transport between jurisdictions, from a county jail to a state prison, or a state prison to a federal prison, the murderer is also between the different notification systems for each jurisdiction. If the prisoner escapes during such a transport, the survivor is not likely to be notified in a timely manner. Ironically, transport is one of the most common times for prisoners to attempt escape.

Automated victim notification systems are not always accurate in their notices and sometimes re-traumatize survivors. For example, one morning a survivor who had testified years earlier against her son's murderer came home to see the light blinking on the answering machine. She hit play and listened to an automated voice notification. "This message is from the victim information and notification system." The voice spelled out this mother's worst nightmare, "Prisoner S...M...I...T...H.... has been released as of today May 3, 2002." Smith was her son's murderer who was serving 25 years to life in prison. She panicked. Between not having a PIN number and not understanding how to navigate the VINE phone menu system, it took hours to get additional information regarding the release message. As it turns out, the murderer was simply being transferred from a county jail to a state correctional facility.

The automated notification system informs those registered in the VINE system whenever prisoners escape, are released, or transferred. Unfortunately, the voice messages do not distinguish release to freedom from release to another correctional facility. The system only tells when the prisoner leaves one facility. The notification system does not contact to confirm that the prisoner has arrived at the proper receiving facility. Although survivors can call and track down this information, it would make more sense for the system to simply modify its message content to avoid setting off false alarms.

Many victim notification programs are separate and distinct from parole board notifications. You may need to register with both the victim notification system and the parole board if you want to be notified of upcoming parole board hearings. In some states and jurisdictions, survivors are allowed to attend parole board meetings to share their input regarding parole, while in other states and jurisdictions, parole boards do not allow the survivor to attend but will accept written parole block statements. Victim and survivor input can make a huge difference in the outcome of parole hearings. The more people expressing an interest in the case, the harder it gets for the parole board to misplace their compassion and forgiveness and play Russian roulette with the lives of innocent people. All murderers learn from their mistakes. Some learn never to kill again. Others learn how to get away with killing better. Too many murderers are released back into society after serving minimal time in jail.

Survivors often organize letter writing campaigns to parole boards protesting the release of a specific prisoner. There are networks of survivors and victim advocates who offer support with their ready pens. Once the murderer comes up for parole, parole board hearings can take place as often as every two years. Every two years the survivor has to revisit the murder to fight parole.

Murderers being released from prison in less than ten years, some in less than five, is not unusual. All too often, sentences assure that the murderers are more likely to reach a point where they are able to move on freely with their lives and forget about what they did, or worse, repeat it, while the survivors of murder victims are never allowed to forget. If not reminded by the fact that their loved one is still just as dead as the day they were murdered, then they are reminded by the trial system, the prison system, the parole system, and the murderer's continued existence and impact on their lives. Dealing with the murderer and whether he/she may go free, if they are already free, and what they will do when they are free becomes one of the *most important issues* in your life. The murder is never over and the process never stops revisiting you to drag you through the horror one more time, until the murderer is dead or you are dead. The fight for justice continues far beyond the verdict.

CHAPTER FIFTEEN

Death as Punishment

Strong, valid, and understandable arguments exist on both sides of the death penalty issue. This chapter does not explore any of these arguments because this book is about the fate of murder victim survivors, not the fate of murderers. The death penalty is a conflict imposed upon our society by murderers, not survivors. The murderers are the ones that committed such cruel and heinous acts of evil that society has to consider whether it is safe to let them live. Without murderers, there would be no debate. When the unresolved issues of a murderer's fate divide the innocent and lead them to turn their backs on their compassion for one another, the murderer wins and everyone else loses.

The death penalty issue can be a very divisive and emotionally volatile topic for murder victim survivors whether they are pro- or anti-death penalty. For some, the issue is black and white, and for others it is gray. All murder victim survivors internalize the death penalty debate on one level or another, even if their loved one's murderer is not facing the death penalty. If you have ever wished the murderer dead, you are facing the death penalty issue.

No matter what a survivor's opinion is on the death penalty, they need and deserve support and validation as much as any other survivor. Survivors should not be pigeonholed as deserving or non-deserving, admirable or non-admirable based upon their opinions and feelings about an issue that our society as a whole cannot agree upon. When the death penalty spotlight shines on a survivor, they either get bashed by the anti-death penalty advocates or bashed by the pro-death penalty advocates. It is a no-win situation.

Survivors are often in an intense emotional state following the murder. It can be extremely painful to hear opinions that differ from their own regarding what should happen to the murderer. On some innate archetypal level, it feels like the destiny of the murderer should be at the mercy of the survivor above and beyond anyone else because the survivors are the people most impacted by the murder. In fact, in some cultures, the justice system revolves around carrying out the survivors chosen punishment. But in most countries, the reality is that survivors do not have much control or input into the matter.

Survivors sometimes find themselves engaged in a debate they did not invite and for which they are not emotionally prepared. Murder victim survivors are sometimes asked how they feel about the death penalty issue only to be verbally attacked if their opinion differs from that of the inquirer or told their opinion is not valid or beyond understanding. If pushed a little too far, it is easy for survivors to slide off the edge of defensiveness and really lose their cool, as the cage rattler points their finger in disgust and shouts, "hate filled fanatic" or "look at the murderer lover." Instead of recognizing that the death penalty issue is emotionally loaded for the survivor, many extremists become more harsh and judgmental about the issue with survivors.

The confrontative attitudes of extremists reveal an undercurrent of assumptions and stereotypes regarding murder victim survivors. Prior to the murder, if you were pro-death penalty and were asked your opinion, you would be just another Joe Schmoe with an opinion on a volatile issue. But if you are pro-death penalty after your loved one has been murdered, now you are a hate-filled person bent on revenge. If you are anti-death penalty after the murder, then you are accused of betraying your loved one and endangering public safety by not advocating for execution. "Surely, if you really loved your murdered child, you would want the murderer dead, right?" Wrong! The death penalty issue has nothing to do with measuring love for the victim.

The only sure thing regarding the death penalty is that murder victim survivors, whether they are for or against the death penalty, have a right to their opinion without being harassed. Verbal attacks by death penalty extremists are not worth the breath they take to deliver. If critics were really interested in what survivors think and feel about the death penalty, they would ditch the attitude and simply listen. Activists who target murder victim survivors with their arguments or pressure murder victim survivors to be spokespersons on the issue are not appropriate. If survivors want to discuss the death penalty issue, they will bring it up and come forward to advocate their position. There are enough survivors on both sides of the issue that welcome opportunities to share their position on the death penalty and explore it through debate. There is no excuse for extremists bothering survivors who simply want to be left alone with their opinions on this issue.

CHAPTER SIXTEEN

The Old War on Terrorism

On Sept. 11, 2001, my grief, my rage, and my fear over my own brother's murder was multiplied by thousands and immersed into the sea of losses that the victims, survivors, and the American community suffered at the hands of evil and terrorism. I think about the people who died a fiery death, like my brother, in those burning buildings. Just like my brother, they made it within one arm's reach of the door. They wanted to live, but did not survive. Anyone who has lost a loved one to violence has a pretty clear understanding of what the emotional aftermath is and will be for the thousands upon thousands of survivors of the victims.

The events of Sept. 11 brought America as a society more in touch with the feelings every murder victim survivor experiences. The cry for justice and the cry for safety are now known from sea to shining sea. I validate and am behind America in pulling up terrorism by its roots, delivering justice, and doing whatever is necessary to stop this from happening to anyone else. But we also need to take in a broader view of terrorism if we truly hope to enjoy a safe and peaceful society. The war on terrorism must extend beyond the focus of international political terrorism. We need the same level of commitment and dedication to eradicating violence that occurs domestically every day in our country. Our policemen need to take the war against murder as seriously as our soldiers take the war against terrorism.

Although this war has been dubbed the "New War On Terrorism," there is nothing new about the murders of Sept. 11. Murder and violence have existed since the beginning of human time. Approximately 3000 lives were lost on Sept. 11. Each year for the past 30 years, there have been from 12,658 to 23,271 murders in this country alone (Maguire and Pastore, p. 308). It is not safe to walk on some streets in our country. People get killed just going about their lives. There are people living in fear. and there are murderers wandering free. The personal and collective impact of the murders that occur one by one every day is every bit as devastating as the mass murders of Sept. 11. To those who have lost a loved one to murder, the only thing that really changed on Sept. 11 was that America as a nation finally understood the impact of murder due to evil and tragic loss.

Many of the national and global responses to the mass murders of Sept. 11 mirror the traumas and struggles that survivors of individual murders experience. America got scared, started to trade freedom for security, and began to restrict their lives to feel safe. America became wary and cautious. America became angry beyond words at the murderers and angry at anyone supporting them. Productivity suffered. The economy dropped and shifted dramatically to pump resources into defense. America got lost in the "what if's," the shame, and the blame looking for the answer to the question, "Why?" America feels betrayed by those who failed to protect our innocent citizens from known terrorists that were in our country. America wants justice and accountability. America wants to make sure this never happens to anyone else again. All murder victim survivors want this assurance.

Many murder victim survivors have struggled to understand the disparity between how our country has responded to the mass murders of Sept. 11 and how it responds to the individual murders that occur every day. Many murder victim survivors admit to some resentment that comparable resources and support were not available to them after the murder of their loved one. They resent that the community did not rally for justice when their loved one was murdered. When just one person is murdered, there are no relief funds like what were raised for the victims and survivors of the World Trade Center, although the economic impact of a single murder on a single family can be just as devastating. When only one person is murdered, survivors are not offered college scholarships as were the survivors of Sept. 11. When just one person is murdered, investigative staffing is not adjusted to respond promptly, thoroughly, and persistently to the urgency of the case. However, considering that the mass murder of Sept. 11 was treated as an act of war, comparisons are not entirely fair.

Envying the aid and support received by the Sept. 11 survivors is misused energy. The World Trade Center survivors deserve all the support the community can give them, just like the survivors of individual murders need support instead of stigmatization. Survivors can only bring the disparity to the attention of the public and ask "why can't we take all murders this seriously?" Over half a million people have been murdered on American soil at the hands of our own citizens in the past the 30 years. Many survivors hope that Sept. 11, 2001, will be the beginning of a new era in how our society responds to violence in all forms.

As a murder victim survivor predating Sept. 11, 2001, I have often wondered: How would America respond if our authorities failed to thoroughly investigate these "plane crashes"? Imagine them leaving leads unfollowed, failing to collect pertinent evidence, failing to question pertinent witnesses, or failing to protect the crime scenes of these "plane crashes"? How would America react if after a day or so, the authorities simply said it was an accident because they did not want to invest the resources necessary to prove otherwise? How would America react if the surviving terrorists were arrested but released on bail until their trial? How would America react if the United States plea-bargained with Osama Bin Laden and his associates and reduced their charges because the court was overbooked? How would America react if our tax dollars paid for not just one attorney, but a team of attorneys, to do everything in their power to aid and abet Osama Bin Laden in derailing justice on some legal-bureaucratic technicality? What if the team argued that the prosecution was reacting to two coincidental accidents by demonizing a man who was not even in the country when it happened? How would America react if the live footage of the planes deliberately flying into the World Trade Center was deemed inadmissible in court because it could emotionally bias the jury, while the defense attorneys argued that the plane crashes were not intentional? How would America react if the charges were dropped because the actual perpetrators died in the plane crashes, making any further investigation a moot effort? How would America react if Bin Laden was found innocent on grounds of insanity because he convinced a jury that he was the victim of American CIA brainwashing years ago? How would America react if the system allowed a terrorist to be made out to be a victim? How would America react if months and then years went by with seemingly no response to the World Trade Center terrorism and no arrests. Then one day, the case simply got filed in the cold case cabinet? How would America react if Osama Bin Laden were tried and convicted, but the sentences for the 3,000 murdered lives were concurrent instead of consecutive because all the deaths stemmed from one act? How would America feel if Osama Bin Laden were granted parole in six years for good behavior while in prison? How would America feel if Bin Laden was handled irresponsibly while in custody, being transported from correctional facility to correctional facility with untrained, unarmed, privately-contracted guards and then he escaped? How would America react if when they voiced their dissatisfaction with this system, they were essentially told to ditch the sour grapes and move on with their lives? Here within the United States, these scenarios more closely resemble the reality that too many murder victim survivors are forced to tolerate on a case-by-case basis.

Here we are, the United States, waging war against any entity harboring, supporting, financing, or training terrorists. Yet within our own country, those helping murderers evade justice through silence, lies, and refuge are rarely pursued with any seriousness. In fact, there are many examples where the criminal justice system itself seems to function as a supporter of the criminal, looking out for their every right to the extent that the principles of justice simply get perverted. Certainly if a murder victim survivor were to put a $25 million bounty on the head of their loved one's murderer and say, "Give me the murderer dead or alive," as President Bush has said, we would be condemned as vengeful, hateful people and we would probably end up in jail for conspiracy to murder.

I am in favor of the swift, thorough, and powerful response our government and law enforcement agencies have had to the Sept. 11 murders. We need more of this level of dedication to solving violent crimes and effecting justice for every victim. We need to bring some consistency to our response to the worldwide cry for justice and the cries for justice that we hear every day for atrocities committed by the hands of our own citizens. Protecting us from the individual murderers who live freely among us and collectively murder 15,000 to 20,000 each year is just as important to our public safety as catching those that murdered 3,000 people on Sept. 11. Mass murder and individual murder evolve from the same evil.

I also hope that the United States as an entity can walk the line that distinguishes us from the perpetrators of terrorism as well as I have seen individual murder victim survivors walk that line. I hope as a government the insight, introspection, and willingness to spiritually and morally grapple with the impulses of fear and rage are not lost, because that is where the war on violence is ultimately fought. If we are truly dedicated to the cause of eradicating terror, we have to look and act domestically as well as worldwide. As King Solomon (635-577 BC) said, "Justice will only be achieved when those who are not injured by crime, feel as indignant as those who are." The war on terrorism will be lost if it stops short of addressing the terror that *every* murder inflicts on the victims, the survivors, and the community. A single murder stuns a family and community to the degree that 3000 murders in a single coordinated assault stunned the world.

CHAPTER SEVENTEEN

Another Kind of Knowing

Multitudes of murder victim survivors will confide that they had uncanny feelings, coincidences, thoughts, dreams, foreshadowings, and even waking visions preceding and surrounding their loved one's death. Some survivors sense their loved one's presence, see them, hear them, have visions or dreams of them, and receive signs and symbols from them. Like a lace curtain flowing in the breeze, the veil that separates this world from the next briefly parts, and messages pass between realms. If we are honored and open to receive them, we experience another kind of knowing—something which transcends our world, something extraordinary and spiritual.

If we are not accustomed to having transcendent experiences, we may feel taken by surprise, freaked out, burdened, or even scared. Faith in our ability to interpret our transcendent experiences accurately does not come overnight. Initially, we may question our own credibility. "Am I creating these experiences to soothe my grief? Are these experiences trauma related? Or, perhaps just daydreams? Meaningless fleeting thoughts? Freak coincidences? Am I crazy, or did something very extraordinary and rare just happen? Although these experiences are very real to me, are they real for anyone else?" Could these feelings of psychic connectedness just be phantom sensations like the leg that still hurts after it has been amputated? Our loved one is gone, but we still feel their presence. Or, are these experiences real and genuine connections with our loved one in the absence of their physical presence?

The answers to these questions are very personal and unique and will reflect our faith and spiritual beliefs. No human being can answer these questions with any more authority than the next. It all boils down to the specific beliefs that we filter our experiences through. Psychic ability in its simplest form is just an openness, a willingness to believe that contact with our deceased loved one and the spiritual world is possible and plausible. The more we believe in a continuing and co-existing spiritual realm, the more experiences in life we are likely to attribute to interactions with the spiritual world. There are whole cultures of human beings that do not even have words to distinguish real from ethereal, or real from imaginary. They view the physical and spiritual worlds as seamless. You may want to consider whether you really need to label your experience as being "real" or "not real" at all. Sometimes a willingness to acknowledge and consider your experience is all that is needed to make the experience meaningful and helpful.

Deciphering the meaning and purpose of our transcendent experiences can become an integral part of our grieving as we strive to integrate the experience on a cognitive, emotional, and spiritual level. Our reactions to our grief and our reactions to the transcendent event become intertwined. Believing in a continued connection with our deceased loved one is an incredible source of comfort and strength, but also a deep emotional risk. If the unfolding of our own lives and deaths proves our beliefs to be unfounded and nothing more than a fantasy, will we be able to deal with that letdown? Will we survive the pain of having the bandages of our faith ripped from our wounds?

When these transcendent experiences occur amid death and loss, we are already in a state of shock, crisis, and intense grief. Amid this confusion and emotional overload, we have to decide whether to share our experience with others or keep it private. We also have to consider to what extent our transcendent experiences should influence our actions. "If I have an intense feeling that something horrible is going to happen to someone, should I tell them?" "Should I tell my wife that I witnessed our son's murder in a dream?" "Should I tell the police where to look for evidence based on a vision of the murderer's actions at the crime scene?"

Sometimes it is our transcendent experiences that first clue us in to the possibility that a murder has taken place. We may smell and feel evil in the air, or just intuitively know that something is amiss beyond the death of our loved one. The more seriously we take our transcendent experiences, the more credibility we risk losing with others if they do not believe us or if the unfolding of events proves our intuitions erroneous. Nobody wants to be tagged "the boy who cried murder." Fear of losing credibility with others can compound feelings of isolation. No matter how intensely we feel, it is very difficult to go to the police or to others and mutter the word "murder" when it is based upon hunches, feelings, and dreams.

Some survivors may fear their transcendent experiences are signs of insanity or emotional weakness. The transcendent experience alone says nothing of your mental health. Your reaction to these experiences speaks more of your mental wellness. Knowing that precognitive experiences related to the death of your loved one are not uncommon is important. Many people have them. Examples are easy to come by when talking among survivors.

A 9-year-old girl tells her mother that she is afraid she is going to be kidnapped and murdered. In previous days, her mother had independently experienced an impending sense of danger and evil, but she did not understand where this feeling was coming from or what to do about it. One month later, the 9-year-old girl and her 16-year-old sister are abducted and brutally murdered by two men.

A 5-year-old girl wakes up on a Tuesday morning crying and pleading with her father, "Please don't go to work today, Daddy. Just don't go. Stay with me." The conversation regresses to hysterical begging. He goes to work because he has to for his job. Two hours later, a plane hijacked by suicidal terrorists crashes into the building where he works. He does not come home that night. His body is never found.

A young woman preparing to move out-of-state confides to her best friend, "I am afraid that if I leave, something horrible will happen, such as my parents' house will burn down, and I'll be returning for a funeral or something like that. It's probably just moving anxiety, but I can't seem to shake the feeling." Three weeks after the move, her brother is murdered in an arson-homicide that destroys their parents' home.

A woman leaves for a vacation to China with her boyfriend. Her sister, who chose not to take the trip, is haunted by the feeling that she will never see her sister again. She feels intense regret for not going with her. During her sister's absence, she experiences an overwhelming panic attack at work and leaves early. Hours later she learns that her sister is missing in China. The following day she learns her sister's murdered body has been found.

Our precognitions are only revealed to us as reality unfolds one moment into the next. Precognition is not the jump-start on reality that it is cracked up to be. The messages usually are not save-the-day material. While many types of precognitive experiences can leave us with positive affirmative feelings, precognitions of murder and violence can extract pure dread from the marrow of our bones. At the same time, the exact meaning of the experience can be incredibly fuzzy and subtle to us. Sometimes we do not even realize information has been imparted to us until the event that makes the message significant occurs. When murder is the revealing event that brings sense to our precognitive experiences, it is chilling, unnerving, and deeply frightening.

Somewhere in the core of our beings we knew something awful was going to happen. We knew. How? Why? "Was the precognitive experience something coming from me, to me, or through me? Could I have used this information differently, such as acting on it instead of dismissing it, or talking about it instead of keeping it secret? Could I have saved my loved one's life?" When things that we think about actually occur, we may wonder, "If I hadn't thought about this happening, would it have happened? Am I responsible somehow? What should I be doing with this knowledge now?"

Whether these transcendent experiences come in the form of a poignant dream, an uncanny coincidence, a daydream or vision, an apparition, or simply an intense feeling, we have to process the experience somehow—even if processing means dismissing it or stuffing it until we are in a less vulnerable state. When we initially experience transcendent phenomenon, it is hard to know what to make of it or what to do with it. The messages we receive are not always clear, but the feelings evoked in us usually are. Transcendent experiences may leave us with an extraordinary sense of encouragement, comfort, worry, dread, confusion, vulnerability, or peace. Transcendent experiences can be fleeting, persistent, or haunting. They do not always come when we invite them and sometimes they visit upon us whether we welcome them or not.

Contemplating the purpose behind our transcendent experiences is critical. Ultimately, the meaning we assign to the event will influence how the event impacts us. For example, if we attribute our transcendent experience to emotional weakness or a mental meltdown, we may feel ashamed or self-conscious of these phenomenon and hold them secret. Keeping such intense experiences secret compounds feelings of isolation.

If we believe the purpose of the event was to alert us so we could intervene and save our loved one's life, and our loved one is now dead, we may experience tremendous feelings of failure and guilt. It is not unusual to struggle with what we "should have" done with the knowledge. When coupled with survivors' guilt, a precognitive thought or dream can transform into a weapon of vicious self-blame.

Sometimes changing the course of someone else's free will is not up to us, even if that will is deeply dangerous and hurtful. Sometimes the purpose of a precognitive experience is simply to prepare us for what is to come. This is why people think ahead and plan—to prepare for what is to come. A precognitive thought is no different. It just reaches into the future on a slightly different level. Foreshadowing can consciously and subconsciously prepare us for what is coming. The degree of shock and trauma we experience may be altered by virtue of the foreshadowing, so when the murder actually occurs, we are better able to function, think clearly, act, offer support, and survive.

If we believe the transcendent experience is a glimpse of evil intended solely to horrify us and control us with fear, our reaction to the event may be terror, reckless defiant fearlessness, or simple denial or dismissal of the transcendent event. Even if we channel our energies proactively into safety and protection, how do we stop these visitations from hell and protect ourselves from this amorphous intrusive evil that we feel or see but cannot change? If you are feeling haunted, building a fence around your backyard or putting a gun in your bedstand will not help you sleep better at night.

Homicidal grief leaves us in a vulnerable state. Our energy is being absorbed by grief. We are in shock. The horror of the murder has traumatized us. We are in emotional and spiritual crisis. Survivors are easy targets for the psychic intrusions of evil. Even if it is your weakest moment, spiritual bravery is a must. Spiritual bravery is the ability to see through terror so you can do what you need to do to protect and take care of yourself and your family. Spiritual bravery also entails talking yourself out of terror when you are lost in it. Evil is very much attracted to fear. Spiritual bravery will help you call out loud to all that is good in the universe and talk back to the evil intrusions upon your psyche.

If you are having transcendent experiences that leave you feeling terrified and powerless, recognize these intrusions for what they are—remnants of someone else's murderous evil acts that you are purging from the fine silk of your psyche. Do not let your fear give more power to evil than it deserves. Evil deserves none. Protection against these psychic intrusions comes through fortifying ourselves spiritually and calling to powers greater than ourselves for help. All the strength you reach for will be yours if you keep reaching and calling for all that is good.

Not all transcendent experiences are scary. We may feel our loved one's presence accompanied by overwhelming feelings of love, peace, joy, and exaltation in the same day that we learn the brutal details of their murder. Transcendent experiences can feel extremely out of place and incongruent with our grief and the horrifying circumstances surrounding our loved one's death. But perhaps there is a reason behind the contrast of grief and exaltation that your loved one's spiritual presence brings. One thought is that the purpose of such visitations is to convey an understanding of continued existence and to offer a piece of the comfort and escape from pain that was given to our loved one by the grace of God, the nature of human consciousness, or the mercy of death.

Continued existence and freedom from suffering are hopes often reaffirmed by our transcendent experiences. What the body experiences versus what the soul experiences are two different truths. It is possible that survivors experience more pain in the aftermath of murder than their loved one did in the process of dying. Perhaps one purpose behind these transcendent experiences is to let us know our loved one is okay, so we can be okay too. If we believe the purpose of our transcendent experiences is to offer evidence of a deep connection to our loved one, a connection that transcends the veil of mortality, we will feel re-affirmed in our faith and our belief in the continued existence of both our loved one and ourselves. We may feel both awestruck and humbled by the immense universe that lies just beyond our sight and grasp.

There are also survivors who experience no transcendent phenomenon. Sometimes there is relief in this, and at other times, a feeling of compounded loss. "Why not me? I want to see my loved one too. I want visions. I want dreams. I want to smell my mother's perfume mysteriously waft through the room. Why do other people experience visitations and connections to their deceased loved one and I don't?" It makes our loved one seem even farther away from us. Just as there are reasons for visitations and communications to occur, there are also many, many plausible reasons why they do not occur or are imperceptible to us.

Transcendent experiences are often subtle, out-of-the-corner-of-your-eye type stuff, but poignant when noticed. Overlooking the signs can be easy. Grief blinds us. We may hold on to our old definitions of our loved one so tightly that it becomes impossible for us to recognize them in any other form. Or, in the earliest phases of grief, perhaps the need to constantly remind ourselves that they are dead blocks us from the experience of their continued existence. We are so busy looking for what is missing that we may not recognize the ways that our loved ones are communicating with us. We communicate with other realms through signs, symbols, timing, and energy. Another kind of knowing does not come to us in the direct manner through which we usually acquire information. By nature, deciphering the meaning of our transcendent experiences is a highly personal and interpretative task.

Some people are extremely psychically adept and have a keen awareness of the spiritual world about them. Yet, often these trained and gifted individuals cannot communicate with their own loved one in the wake of death. When grief is gushing out from our depths, we long so strongly for those we miss that all our energies form a one-way road reaching outward. The longing pulls us further and further away from ourselves. The longing creates a vacuum in our hearts. We become self-absorbed in our grief and alienated from the ebb and flow of the world around us. While in this state, the emotional current of our grief may be too strong for our loved one to navigate with their newly transformed energies.

Transcendent experiences also may compel us to consider the concepts of destiny and fate. If I had precognitions, then my brother's demise was a plan unfolding long in advance of his actual murder. How could such horror ever be intentionally woven into the divine fabric of the unfolding universe? Were our loved ones destined to become murder victims? Was that part of their purpose on earth? Perhaps the murder was the end result of an evil ripple in the universe that was destined to meet with a victim. Your loved one was that victim. Destiny was in operation, but so was free will. Murder was one possible destiny that could have unfolded. Murder is the destiny that the killer chose for our loved one. Murder is a choice. Murder is the outcome of a murderous act. It is the theft, the anti-creation of our loved one's life destiny. Murder is never a divinely-given destiny.

CHAPTER EIGHTEEN

Letting Go of Despair

There is nothing complicated about despair. It is simply misery without hope. Despair is a normal emotional response to loss and experiences of powerlessness, and it has the potential of growing into a chronic self-perpetuating state of being. Despair grows like an invasive vine. It weaves around and around us, choking us off from the promise of life, binding us tighter and tighter to our pain. Beyond this, the only thing anyone really needs to know about despair is how to let go.

Times of misery are inevitable, but we do not have to wed our misery to hopelessness forever. Despair comes upon us without asking, just as the murder of our loved one did. But despair does not really hold onto us, we hold onto it. Reclaiming your life from despair is not about fighting and defending yourself from sadness, but rather about letting go and letting in—letting go of what hurts and letting in what heals. Amazingly, something as passive as letting go and letting in can be difficult even for people who desperately want to feel good again.

Letting go of despair involves first learning to let ourselves grieve. You have to allow yourself to cry before you can stop crying. The best way to assure that you can have times when you do not cry is to allow yourself time when you can cry. Many people are afraid that if they let the tears come, they will not be able to stop and they will die crying. Indulging your grief does not mean that sadness and anguish have to be the beginning, middle, and end of your story or your murdered loved one's story. Tears are easier to manage if you think of them as something that we let come and we let go, rather than something we have to fight back for fear of having our lives washed away. If you have the strength to let the tears come, you will also find the strength to let them go. Trust yourself, trust nature, and trust God. Tears serve us on many levels

—physiological, psychological, and spiritual. Tears were created to accompany the most intense and emotionally significant moments of our lives. They are a tribute to the things that really matter to us and the things that we really care about. If we did not care, we would not cry.

Our culture is pretty uncomfortable with grief and fairly stingy about how much grieving we allow people to do within the bounds of social acceptability. Many people go through life feeling ashamed of their grief because our culture treats it like something we complete and recover from, something that has an end. When we fail to achieve that elusive myth called closure, we introject and project the failures of grief upon ourselves and those who continue to grieve with us. If we were to publicly wail and keen like folks do in some countries, we would be taken to the doctor's office, medicated, and treated for depression and anxiety. Consequently, there are a lot of people out there with chronic unresolved grief who try to treat it with everything but the act of grieving. If we allowed ourselves to do some high-powered wailing, maybe we would not have so many people trying to compensate for grief, withdraw from life, and crowd out their sorrows with unhealthy behaviors and attitudes years upon years upon years after their losses. Maybe we would not have so many people in pain.

The best thing you can do for yourself and your loved one is to ignore the social morays as much as you can get away with and understand that grief has no end. Love knows no bounds and neither does grief. We do not stop loving people just because they are not right here with us. Denying your grief would be like denying your love. A world that denies love is nothing but fertile ground for despair to take root. Letting yourself grieve fully is a way of letting yourself love fully and also a way of warding off chronic despair.

Just as grieving is an act of love for the dead, healing is an act of love for the living. Letting go of despair involves letting yourself do both. Healing is a commitment to yourself to find a way to be okay, even better than okay, no matter how long it takes to get there. Healing from grief *never* means not grieving. Healing simply means letting yourself live. We do not recover from grief, we change how we cope with it. Healing in its simplest form is change. It involves facing, overcoming, and reducing pain so we can enjoy living more. The only way to heal from grief is to face it with courage and self-compassion and let it transform you. The emotional and spiritual stretching and reaching inherent in remembering, honoring, and longing for what we love can ultimately bring us to grow toward what we love or even grow into what we love.

Letting go of despair involves learning to let in hope. Most non-negotiable losses are followed by bouts of hopeless despair. Death and tragedy have a way of bringing our vulnerability and powerlessness full-faced before us. The overwhelming sense of personal fragility that comes with this confrontation naturally evokes feelings of helplessness and hopelessness. What is the point in building relationships and bonds with others when all it takes is one instantaneous act of evil or destruction to take the people we love the most away from us in the worst imaginable ways? What is the point in building dreams to chase when life can sweep the legs out from under us at any time, rendering both the dream and the chase obsolete? When someone dies, the statute of limitations on hope is up. We lose every hope we once held for our deceased loved one and every hope we shared with them.

Survivors may lose trust in their ability to safeguard their most cherished dreams and emotional investments. Losing this self-trust changes everything. The meaning of hope suddenly shifts from "more to love and enjoy" to "more to lose." We may doubt the reasonableness of the hopes we once held. Hope becomes a costly gamble we cannot afford instead of a shot at something really worthwhile and good for us. Hope is the currency of our faith. If we are only willing to invest it in sure bets, we are grossly devaluing its benefits to our lives and well-being. Hopes and prayers are often one and the same. If your spirit feels too flattened to hope—pray. If you have no energy to pray, just be still and sit with the one you pray to. Breathe and feel the blessings that enter your life with every breath.

The better we understand hope, the easier it becomes to let it re-enter our lives. Hope is the ability to picture and pre-experience aspects of our dreams and aspirations independent of the odds for or against them actually coming to fruition in reality. Even though hope is the opposite of despair, the driving force of hope and grief are ironically the same. Both hope and grief involve an intense longing, very much like unrequited love. In a way, grief is a hope turned backward in time. Most survivors experience periods of intense longing for the way things were or for things to be different than they are. We may wish, hope, and fantasize that our loved one is still with us. The more intensely we experience and envision the hopes of grief, the more intensely we ache when the reality dawns and re-dawns on us. "My child is not coming back."

As the hopes of grief fall hard upon reality over and over again, disappointment and heartbreak become the recurring themes of wishing for things that are not and simply cannot be. Longing becomes painful to us, and we start pulling up lame on all our hopes. Despair circles like a vulture waiting for our hope to stumble and collapse face down on the arid plain of grief. Even when hope falls, it is by no means dead. Even if hope lies motionless on the ground for years, it is not dead. Hope and grief are both made of longing. If you have the capacity to grieve, then you also have the capacity to hope.

What do we dare hope for in a world that can arbitrarily strip our lives of all we love in an instant? Our capacity for hope is expanded through the repeated asking and answering of this question. When building our capacity for hope, we may need to start small. Grief consumes a lot of energy. It is normal to feel like you barely have enough energy to keep breathing much less fabricate hopes. Start with hopes that require only seconds of effort and can come into being within a single day or even a single moment. "I hope to find a reason to laugh today. I hope to find a reason to smile." "I hope to see something beautiful today." "I hope to carry out at least one work of love today." Do not just *say* your hopes, envision them. A mental picture takes but a second or two. Imagine the tickle of a good belly laugh. Imagine the momentary connection of a smile returned. Imagine being stunned by the emanating beauty of the sunset. Imagine the rush of warmth that the giving of a simple kindness can bring. Imagine your loved one in exalted beauty.

The more we let in the world around us, the harder and harder it becomes to hold onto despair. Letting in the world is not a passive act by any means. We have to notice the world if we are to let it in.

Opening up requires mindfulness. Mindfulness also helps protect us from letting in the things of this world that can hurt us. The best way to realize a hope is to notice it manifesting in the world around you. If you hope to smile, notice smiles. If you hope to laugh, notice laughter. If you hope to witness beauty, notice beauty. If you hope to give, notice what others might need or want. It only takes a second or two to notice something. It is okay to interrupt your despair long enough to notice things that are beautiful or comforting to you—flowers flourishing from the cracks in the sidewalk, a withered old man whose face lights up with a smile, a leaf twirling to the ground, a kitten jumping after a fly, a metal spoon on a solid wood table, the smell of coffee brewing, bread baking, or bacon frying. Notice the little things. Notice how they make you feel, and if it feels good, take another moment and notice it again. Then bless the moment with your gratitude and let it go, being certain not to forget to ask the question, "Why?"

Mindfulness does not come easy when our minds are stuck in the horrors that have touched our lives. Intrusive images of murder and feelings of grief and rage often take center stage in our consciousness and steal our concentration from the here and now. Overcoming despair involves purging these dark images from the center stage of our psyche. The key is noticing and creating a life to replace your despair. The challenge is finding the strength and energy to do the work.

Murder is the diabolical dirty bomb of anti-creation, an implosion of evil that sucks the life out of everything it touches. Murder's noxious wake of anti-energy poisons the drive to create and nurture, deadening all the things that help us to feel alive. Growing out of this life-sucking void of despair involves detoxifying ourselves from murder's paralytic poison. There is no magic anti-serum. The only way to eliminate despair is to fill it with something healthier. Fill the darkness with light.

Create something. Nurture something. Plant a garden. Paint a picture. Write a line of poetry. Hold another human being in your arms. Help someone. No matter how much your will is lacking, *do it anyhow.* Your will has been poisoned and you simply cannot depend upon it to lead you out of despair. Creative energy is something that flows through us more than from us. Creating does not take as much energy as you might think at first. When you are so thoroughly consumed with grief that you cannot even find the desire to wake up in the morning, creating and nurturing may seem like an insurmountable task. But if you can find the strength and tenacity to open the door a little, you will find that creation has a way of coming in on its own volition if you let it. Nature abhors a vacuum. Wherever there is space, creation of one kind or another will try to fill the void.

Some survivors find it easier to open the door to their creative energy if they somehow integrate their grieving with their creating and nurturing. They may paint a picture of their grief, plant a tree, or write a poem in remembrance and honor of their loved one. Some survivors are amazed at the quality of the works they are able to produce at a time when they feel so pained and depleted. It is not unusual during times of intense pain and angst to find that our creativity brings forth more poignant, inspired, and meaningful symbols and messages. Do not forget: it is your drive to create and nurture that is injured, not your capacity to do so.

When creative and nurturing energy flows through us, it not only reflects what is inside of us, but also cleanses us. Both the beautiful and the ugly come out. Creative expression after violence can be scary. There is nothing pretty about the putrid backwash of murder. Survivors often go through a period of rather dark creation. Their works may reflect the murderous images and feelings of sadness, anger, rage, guilt, and fear that are swirling around inside. Survivors may work with images of what they believe the murderer should suffer or what they believe their loved one suffered. They may fear their dark artwork attests to what they have become. Expressing your experience of the darkness that touched your life does not make you a dark person. Detoxifying from the poison of murder involves expressing these dark feelings and images and getting them outside of yourself before they solidify on the inner walls of your psyche sealing you into a tomb of despair.

Although dark creations may be necessary for some survivors, it is also very healing to parallel and balance the dark creations with other works that evoke feelings of peace, love, and comfort. Some survivors find their creative energies caught for a time in the archetypal battle of good and evil. There is nothing wrong with expressing the emotional and spiritual conflicts of what you are going through. If you paint a picture of your rage, also be sure to paint a picture of your love. The more you create and nurture, the more you will feel alive again. Creating and nurturing are two of many tools available to us to fill the void of despair.

Smiles and laughter are another force of healing we can use to fill the hollowness. They propagate spontaneously. The more we smile, the more others smile at us. The more we laugh, the more others laugh with us. The more laughter we hear, the more we want to laugh. Grief tends to scare laughter and smiles away for a time. One, we are profoundly sad. And two, many people withhold their smiles and laughter because they are afraid of being perceived as inappropriate, inconsiderate, or disrespectful with their humor and happiness. No matter how devastating our loss, we eventually need to let ourselves laugh and smile again, even if just a little, and give others permission to do the same around us.

Survivors may need to be proactive in bringing smiles and laughter back into their lives at first. Do not forget, your will has been poisoned so you may have to seek humor at first, even if you have no real will to laugh. If you do not have the energy to laugh, start small. Commit yourself to finding at least one reason to laugh every day. Buy a joke book or a funny calendar. Peruse a humorous Web site. Watch a comedy show or movie. If you witness something that even remotely strikes you as funny, crack a smile and laugh a little. If you want to make it real simple, just buy a tape of nothing but laughter. Laughter is contagious and can make you laugh even when there is absolutely nothing funny at all to laugh about. Some of the biggest belly laughs are triggered by simply laughing at yourself laughing at nothing at all. If you give yourself permission to laugh, you might be surprised with the belly laughs you can engage in even when immersed in the depths of grief. Laughter will actually give you more energy to face your crisis.

Many survivors recount stories of something tickling their funny bone in the midst of waking and burying their loved one, not being able to stop themselves from laughing, and having the laughter reach such proportions that they were brought to tears once again. These survivors often ask, "Is laughter in the midst of grief disrespectful? I just couldn't help it even though I am profoundly sad." The answer is "no." Laughter and mourning are not mutually exclusive. You can do both. In fact, laughter is very healing and helpful in managing stress and is probably more important to our well-being when we are feeling the worst. Laughter has a way of helping us feel "normal" again even if it only lasts a minute or so. Physiologically, laughter triggers the release of the body's "feel-good" biochemicals. Many people engage in nervous laughter or nervous smiling to counter the chemical imbalances caused by stress and help reset the body's chemistry in much the same way that tears do. Solely speaking from a physiological point of view, the more we laugh, the less we have to cry.

We can also fill the void of despair with learning. There is nothing more empowering than learning something new. Learning seeds change and cultivates the hope that someday you will see and experience your life differently. Many survivors go through a period of intense learning to find ways of getting through the aftermath of murder more gracefully. They may read books, magazine articles, and peruse Web sites soaking up everything available to them about grief, murder, posttraumatic stress disorder, and justice. Others use learning to remove themselves temporarily from their pains and struggles by focusing on learning a skill completely unrelated to murder and grief. Other survivors focus their learning on spiritual questions raised by the loss of their loved one. No matter what you are seeking to learn, learning cannot hurt you. Learning is always a constructive response to crisis and despair.

Despair is nourished by powerlessness and stagnation of spirit. We remain stuck in despair until we believe in our power to change something for ourselves, such as the way we live, the way we interact, or the way we feel. The first principle of change is understanding and accepting the things we cannot change. Although we will never be able to change the source of our pain or the ending of our loved one's life, we can still change our own lives if we are willing to change ourselves. Ironically, changing the one thing most under our control, ourselves, is often the hardest thing of all to do. Change does not occur in leaps but rather in little baby steps that over time carry us far into a new and desired life. Our capacity for change is something we have to exercise and develop. If you cannot change the big things in your life like your attitude and disposition, start with smaller things. Rearrange the furniture, hang new pictures on the wall, try a different route into work, try smiling at someone you usually ignore, try anything that will bring refreshment into your life. I am not suggesting we can solve our problems by simply moving the furniture, but even small changes exercise and strengthen our ability to pull ourselves out of the ruts where stagnation pools.

There may be no such thing as getting over it and moving on, but grieving and pursuing justice should not mean spending every day of the rest of your life spinning your tires in the mire of murder going nowhere. If it does, then you are the one serving the life sentence. Letting go of despair entails learning to turn off the engine and step out of the struggle, even if just for a little while. Turning off the struggle to replenish yourself is not the same as giving up. People are simple, like wells, when it comes to emotional energy and fortitude. If you never turn off the pump, the well runs dry. Building your stores of emotional energy and fortitude are key to overcoming despair. Many survivors debate, "Is it okay to just stop struggling when so much has been lost and so much is at stake?" It is not really a matter of struggling versus not struggling, but rather choosing your struggles wisely and knowing when to rest.

If ceasing to struggle means letting go of the pain because you are too tired to carry it any further, do not struggle. Just let go. If ceasing to struggle means having days when you do not think of death and murder, do not struggle. Let the dark thoughts go. If ceasing to struggle means having days when you choose to be blind to the injustice and cruelty of the world, do not struggle. Spend the day looking at only the things you want to see. If not struggling means lying down when you are tired, laughing when you are sick of crying, or crying when you feel like crying, do not struggle. Let yourself be and trust your intuition about what you need to stop hurting and start living.

If struggling means falling silent and accepting some broken down jalopy being passed off as law and justice, keep struggling. If struggling means exercising the will to reconnect with life, by all means struggle. If struggling means continuing to yearn spiritually and trying to see beyond the veil of mortality to confirm your loved one's continued existence, then keep struggling. If struggling means not giving up on your faith and values, then keep struggling. If struggling means remembering and honoring the people that are important to us, both dead and alive, never stop struggling.

No matter what you do with your life from here, *the murder will never be okay.* You will always feel the way you feel about your loved one's murder, and it will never feel good. You will never forget what happened, whether you want to or not. You will never be able to change what happened to your loved one, but you can change what happens to you. The murder will never be okay, but you can be.

You can heal from the trauma that surrounds your loved one's death. Do not allow the evil that hid behind the human face that smiled at your loved one in one moment and murdered them in the next to control the destiny of your life. You do not have to let murder commandeer your consciousness 24/7. Do not allow the murder to freeze your emotional and spiritual landscape, or stop you from growing and changing with other aspects of your life. Do not let the murder sever you from a continued sense of shared humanity and connectedness with others. Do not let the murder pull you further from your higher power and further from your most fundamental beliefs. Do not be another victim of the murderer—be a survivor.

The ills of the world will always be ill. The beauty of the world will always be beautiful. They do not stop one another from being what they are. Do not let murder stop you from being everything that you are and everything you were meant to be. Your loved one's murder will test everything in you—your love, your strength, your faith, your values, your peace, and your beliefs. May this test become testimony to all that is good in you, all that is good in the world, and all that is good in the heavens.

Forever Changed

I could not write this book again—ever. The person who finished writing this book, is not the same person who started it. The writing of this book changed me, brought me to a brighter threshhold. I hope and pray it does the same for you.

Bibliography

American Psychiatric Association. (1994). *Diagnostic And Statistical Manual of Mental Disorders (DSM-IV)—4th Edition.* Arlington VA: American Psychiatric Association.

Aub, K. A. _(1995). *Children Are Survivors Too: A Guide Book for Young Homicide Survivors.* Boca Raton, FL: Grief Educational Resources Inc.

Henry-Jenkins, W. (1996). *Just Us: Overcoming and Understanding Homicidal Loss and Grief.* Omaha, NB: Centering Corporation.

Jenkins, W. (2001). *What to Do When the Police Leave: A Guide to the First Days of Traumatic Loss.* Richmond, VA: In Sight Books.

Maguire, K. & Pastore, A.L. (Eds.). (2001). *Sourcebook of Criminal Justice Statistics 2000, 28th Edition.* Available online at: www.albany.edu/sourcebook.

Pizzi, W.T. (1999). *Trials Without Truth: Why Our System of Criminal Trials Has Become an Expensive Failure and What We Need to Do to Rebuild It.* New York, NY: New York Univ Press.

Redmond, L.M. (1989). *Surviving: When Someone You Love Was Murdered: A Professional's Guide to Group Grief Therapy for Families and Friends of Murder Victims.* Clearwater, FL: Psychological Consultation.

Robertson, D.P. (2002). *Tears From Heaven, Voices From Hell*, New York, NY: Writers Club Press.

Spungen, Deborah. (1997). *Homicide: The Hidden Victims: A Guide for Professionals.* London, England: Sage Publishing.

U.S. Department Of Justice, Office of Justice Programs. *Bureau Of Justice Statistics.* 2002. Available online at: www.ojp.usdoj.gov/bjs.

Resources Available to Survivors of Murder Victims

Survivor Support

Mothers Against Drunk Driving (MADD)

511 E. John Carpenter Freeway, Suite 700, Irving, TX 75062

(800) GET-MADD / (800) 438-6233 / (972) 869-2206 (fax)

http://www.madd.org

National organization with more than 600 local chapters providing support and advocacy for people who have been affected by drunk driving or underage drinking. Services and resources available include: information regarding legal, medical, and financial issues; discussion forums.

Murder Victims' Families For Reconciliation

2161 Massachusetts Avenue, Cambridge, MA 02140

(617) 868-0007 / (617) 354-2832 (fax)

http://www.mvfr.org

National organization of survivors of murder victims and state killings who oppose the death penalty. Services and resources available include: advocacy for programs and policies that reduce the rate of homicide and promote crime prevention and alternatives to violence; advocacy for programs helping survivors/victims to rebuild their lives.

Parents of Murdered Children (POMC)

100 East Eighth Street, Suite B-41, Cincinnati, OH 45202

(513) 721-5683 / (513) 345-4489 (fax)

http://www.pomc.com

National organization with local chapters providing support for all survivors of murder, not just parents. Services and resources available include: monthly support groups and meetings, victims' advocacy, court accompaniment, second opinion services to provide answers to questions and concerns regarding a death and subsequent investigations, survivors' newsletter, remembrance program, grief weekends, education, training, consultation, murder response team, speaker's bureau, and more.

Victims of Crime Assistance League (VOCAL Foundation)

P.O. Box 16670, San Francisco, CA 94116-6670

(415) 731-9880

http://www.vocal-jmv.org/

Services and resources available include: Trial and courtroom support, information and education about trial and sentencing processes, victim/witness referral service, advocacy, introduction and support of legislation, continual parole monitoring, annual memorial service, and more.

Concerns of Police Survivors (COPS)

P.O. Box 3199 - S. Highway 5, Camdenton, MO 65020

(573) 346-4911 / (573) 346-1414 (fax)

http://www.nationalcops.org

Services and resources available include: Support to survivors through local chapters, counseling programs, retreats, trial and parole support, training, education, and public awareness campaigns.

Online Murder Victim Survivor Support Forums

http://groww.org/community/boards/

The Web site for GROWW which offers a whole community of grief support with something for just about any circumstance. The murder victim survivors' message board is called silenced angels.

http://www.murdervictims.com

Web site designed to offer support and resources to murder victim survivors. Includes a chat room and message board for survivors of murder victims.

http://www.voicesheard.com

Web site that offers interactive forums dealing with a wide range of issues including, violence, justice, law enforcement, and personal healing.

http://www.pomc.com

Web site for POMC (support family members and friends of survivors), which includes interactive online discussion forums for murder victim survivors.

Victims' Advocacy

Tragedy Assistance Program (TAPS)
2001 South Street, N.W., #300, Washington, DC 20009
1-800-959-TAPS
http://www.taps.org/
For survivors of military personnel

National Organization For Victims Assistance (NOVA)
1757 Park Road NW, Washington, DC 20010
(202) 232-6682 24 hours-a-day / (202) 462-2255 (fax)
http://www.try-nova.org

National Center For Victims Of Crime
2000 M Street, NW, Suite # 480, Washington, DC 20036
202-467-8700 / 202-467-8701 (fax) / 1-800-FYI-CALL
http://www.ncvc.org

National Association Of VOCA Administrators
5702 Old Sauk Road, Madison, WI 53705-0006
http://www.navaa.org

National Association of Crime Victim's Compensation Boards
NACVCB, P.O. Box 16003 / Alexandria, VA 22302.
http://www.nacvcb.org/

The National Coalition of Homicide Survivors
Homicide Survivors, Inc.
c/o Pima County Attorney
32 N. Stone, 11th Floor, Tucson, AZ 85701
(520) 740-5729 / (520) 740-5642 (fax)
(520) 881-1794 (Help Line)
http://www.mivictims.org/nchs/index.html

Office for Victims of Crime (OVC)
U.S. Department of Justice / Office for Victims of Crime
    810 7th Street NW, Washington, DC 20531
    (800) 627-6872 / (877) 712-9279

Citizens Against Homicide
    P.O. Box 2115, San Anselmo, CA 94979
    (415) 455-5944 / (415) 454-0298 (fax)
    http://www.murdervictims.com/CAH.htm

Justice For All
    (713) 935-9300
    http://www.jfa.net/index.html

Unsolved Murders and Missing Persons

America's Most Wanted
    P.O. Box CrimeTV, Washington, DC 20016-9126
    http://www2.amw.com
    Television show that profiles cases and helps capture criminals via tips called in by viewers.

National Center for Missing and Exploited Children
    Charles B. Wang International Children's Building
    699 Prince Street, Alexandria, VA 22314
    (703) 274-3900 / (800) THE-LOST
    http://www.missingkids.com
    Services and resources available include: Assistance in recovering missing children; public education designed to help prevent child abduction and exploitation.

The Polly Klaas® Foundation
    P.O. Box 800, Petaluma, CA 94953
    (800) 587-4357 (24-Hour Hotline) / (707) 769-1334
    (707) 769-4019 (fax)
    http://www.pollyklaas.org
    Services and resources available include: Assistance in recovering missing children; public education designed to help prevent child abduction and exploitation.

Sexual Homicide Exchange / Citizens for Case Closure

1730 New Brighton Blvd., #325, Minneapolis, MN 55413

(877) SHE-1444 Montana / (301) 345-9579 Washington, D.C.

(707) 313-1980 (fax)

http://www.she-dc.com

Provides information, education, and victim advocacy. Independently evaluates investigations of homicides and sexual crimes to address concerns of victims/survivors. Facilitates communication between families and law enforcement.

Unsolved Crimes

PMB #144

6338 N. New Braunfels, San Antonio, Tx 78209

(210) 826-4052 / (210) 828-4867

http://www.unsolvedcrimes.com

Investigation of selected long-unsolved murders.

Vidocq Society Case Referrals

1704 Locust Street, Second Floor, Philadelphia, PA 19103

(215) 545-1450

http://www.vidocq.org/seekhelp.html

Investigation of selected long-unsolved murders. All work is done pro bono.

Academic Programs In Victims' Studies

The Victim's Institute, California State University, Fresno

Department of Criminology - Justice Center MS/MF 104

2225 E. San Ramon, Fresno CA 93740-8029

(559) 278-2305 / (559) 278-7265 (fax)

http://www.csufresno.edu/criminology/victimservices.htm

Center On Violence and Victims Studies, Washburn University

1700 SW College Ave., Topeka, KS 66621

(785) 231-1010, Ext. 1399 or 1242 / (785) 231-1028 (fax)

http://www.washburn.edu/ce/jcvvs/

National Crime Victims Research and Treatment Center
Department of Psychiatry and Behavioral Sciences
Medical University of South Carolina
165 Cannon Street, P.O. Box 250852, Charleston, SC 29425
(843) 792-2945 / (843) 792-3388 (fax)
http://www.musc.edu/cvc/

Center for the Study of Crime Victims' Rights,
Remedies, Resources
University of New Haven
300 Orange Avenue, West Haven, CT 06516
(203) 932-7041 / (203) 931-6030 (fax)
http://www.newhaven.edu/california/victims/

American University's Washington College of Law
4801 Massachusetts Ave, NW, Washington, DC 20016-8187
http://www.wcl.american.edu/

Department of Criminal Justice, University of North Texas
359 Chilton Hall, Denton, TX 76203-5130
(940) 565-2562 / (940) 565-2548 (fax)
http://www.unt.edu/cjus/index.htm

Department of Criminology and Criminal Justice
University of Maryland at College Park
Samuel J. LeFrak Hall, University of Maryland
College Park, MD 20742
(301) 405-4699

Other

Restitution Incorporated
106 E Melrose Place / Chapel Hill, NC 27516
(919) 932-7680
http://www.restitutioninc.org/
An organization that promotes healing between offenders and victims
by helping offenders make restitution for their crimes. Services and
resources available include: a forum for offenders to apologize for the
harm they have caused and for victims to share their journeys from
grief to healing

Sample Sentencing Letter

To: Probation Officer Doing Pre-Sentencing Profile and
    Judge Doing the Sentencing

Re: Sentencing of Joe Driver

Dear Justice:

On July 8, 2000, Joe Driver transformed a vehicle into a dangerous weapon when he chose to endanger the lives of countless drivers. This choice took the lives of two young people and injured four other people. A quick look at the circumstances and Joe Driver's history is all it takes to see that it was just matter of time before Joe caused an accident of this magnitude.

Joe has repeatedly driven recklessly, driven under the influence of drugs and alcohol, driven with no license, registration, or insurance. We have systems in place to protect society from people like Joe. This is why his license was suspended, but Joe chose to over-ride these societal protections and drive anyhow. At the time of this tragedy, he was fleeing police because he did not want to be stopped for a suspended license, no insurance, no registration, and he had alcohol and drugs in his system.

A quick look at Joe's behaviors since this tragedy, such as driving while intoxicated only 4.5 months after he killed these two young persons, clearly shows that it is only a matter of time before he kills or hurts more people in this way. Driving under the influence, reckless driving, and endangering the lives of others are merely gambling games to Joe. When people who repeatedly endanger others through negligence and recklessness fail to take the lives of others seriously, fail to respect the limitations that are put on them to protect society, fail to make restitutions, and fail to learn from the horrors they inflict on the lives of other people, our innocent citizens depend upon the justice system to do its duty to protect society through imprisonment.

With some types of criminals, there are steps we can take to reduce our risk of being victimized. We try to secure our homes, not walk alone in unsafe neighborhoods, not get mixed up with violent people, etc. But there is absolutely nothing we can do individually to protect ourselves from people, like Joe Driver, who turn cars into weapons and play Russian roulette with our lives. Maybe Joe did not mean to kill anyone, but he certainly was and still is willing to put anybody's life in danger for his own convenience and nominal gain. This is just one shade shy of a sociopath.

I strongly urge you to uphold the duty of the justice system to protect society from dangerous people and sentence Joe Driver to the maximum allowable sentence.

Sincerely,

Name Of Concerned Citizen

Sample Parole Block Letter

RE: Parole Hearing of Delton Dowthitt

Dear Parole Board Members:

On June 13, 1990, Delton Dowthitt strangled 9-year-old Tiffany Purnhagen so hard with a rope that she was for all intents and purposes decapitated. Meanwhile, Delton's father sexually mutilated and ripped the throat out of Tiffany's 16-year-old sister, Gracie Purnhagen. Delton stated that Gracie had broken up with him and he just snapped—went into a rage. The relationship he is referring to was only a couple weeks in duration and there is some speculation as to whether there was a relationship at all. He has also stated that his father told him they had to kill the girls.

How do we protect ourselves from people like Delton who are willing to kill at someone else's suggestion? What happens the next time someone suggests Delton participate in murder? If this is how Delton handled the break-up of a very short relationship, how will he handle the break-up of a serious relationship? How will he handle a divorce? How will he handle other types of rejection that are an inherent part of life? I say, let us not find out how Delton will handle these situations. I say let us not gamble with innocent lives. I say two dead girls are more than enough to tell us that Delton is a dangerous man. His behavior in prison, violent outbursts and escape attempts, have only reaffirmed the fact that he is still dangerous.

Although this is uncomfortable, I am going to ask you to close your eyes and picture these murders. Picture the rope, picture the terror these girls experienced in their last moments on earth. Picture the type of monster it would take to do this to a 9-year-old girl. Now, put Delton's face on that monster. Close your eyes one more time and picture yourself taking a walk around the block, seeing your new neighbor, Delton, outside working in the

201

yard. Picture him strolling over to the sidewalk, hand extended with a big smile on his face, to introduce himself to you and your children. How will you and your children ever know that behind that face lurks a murderer? How will you protect yourself and your children from the danger you cannot see? The best way to protect the next unsuspecting victim is to eliminate the opportunity and keep Delton behind bars.

Like you, I never knew Gracie, Tiffany, or Delton, but the thought of Delton being paroled after only 11 years fills me with outrage. His crime has not been reduced over the past 11 years, why should his sentence? Gracie and Tiffany's family are still suffering their losses. The thought of Delton EVER being paroled fills me with fear—a fear that is every bit as real as Gracie and Tiffany are dead. Delton was sentenced to 45 years to life to protect society from him and punish him for what he did to Tiffany and Gracie. I implore you not to take that protection and that justice away.

Sincerely,

Carrie M. Freitag

APPENDIX D

Sample Impact Statement

Dear Honorable Justice:

It has been one year, ten months, and 20 days ago since the horrifying murder of my son, Bill. This time has been excruciatingly painful for all of Bill's family—his father, brother, sisters, nephews, friends, and myself. There are no words in any language that can describe the pain, anger, guilt, despair, and loneliness that we have felt as a result of Bill's murder.

When Lawrence Tutt deliberately chose to take Bill's life and set our family home on fire, my life was shattered. I have spent the last two years trying to put my life back together again. But it cannot be done. There are too many pieces missing. Larry not only took my son from me, he also destroyed our home and everything in it—baby books, pictures, childhood drawings, and all the other treasures that meant so much. He took away my son's life as well as the sentimental items that spoke to our family's pride, accomplishments, and love. Larry took our past, our present, and our future.

Larry robbed his best friend—my son—of his life. He took from us a young man whose loving nature, love of life, and giving spirit were an inspiration to all who knew him. He took Bill's dreams and the family he planned to have one day.

Bill was gifted with the ability to relate to others in such a manner that many considered him to be their best friend and trusted confidant. Now I see them floundering in loss and anger, but I am unable to help. I cannot give them any resolve, comfort, or answers. As I live day-by-day lost in my own numbness and emotional pain, Bill is forever in my thoughts. He is in the beauty of the landscape, in nature, and even in the favorite foods which he enjoyed—foods which I can no longer swallow because I know he should be here to savor them too.

Bill had learning difficulties. He could not function effectively within the public school system, but he was self-educated to the point that some people would ask what college he had attended. Bill loved poetry, art, music, reading, and learning about all religions. He had a very strong spiritual belief that showed in how he related with others. He believed a person should be judged for who they are, not by what they have, or what they brag about.

No one will ever be able to read Bill's poetry, see his artwork, or listen to his guitar playing again. Larry Tutt took all that away. It is hard to comprehend that another human being can take another's life, especially one that reached out to help him when no one else would. Lawrence Tutt used my son's friendship for his own selfish endeavors and evil needs.

The night of Dec. 17, 1998, I heard Bill and Larry go upstairs. I heard them talking and laughing before Bill went to sleep. I know that the events leading up to Bill's death, as told by Larry, are false.

I am haunted by the image of Bill going to bed, falling asleep, and feeling secure. He thought that smoke alarms, a sliding glass door for emergency exit, and his trusted dog would protect him. Bill never suspected that Larry would disable all these safeguards that night. Bill had every reason to feel good about himself and his life—he had just started a new job and was looking forward to the Christmas holidays. Instead, he woke up engulfed in flames. The smoke alarms did not sound, the sliding door could not be moved, and his dog did not bark. All because he was betrayed by a man who portrayed himself as a friend.

204

To be burned alive in such a horrific, painful manner has to be the most frightening death there is. I will never get over the guilt I carry for believing Larry's story of being an innocent bystander at the wrong place at the wrong time. In truth, he was guilty of driving a vehicle containing 188 pounds of marijuana. He is so good at deception and lying. He hides behind a facade of manners and charm which he attained from his upbringing. Neither my husband nor I ever knew Larry's parents. We were farmers and they socialized in a completely different social circle. Larry told us he came from Skaneateles Falls and that his parents cared nothing about him. I thought this was true until I learned about the lovely home they owned on East Lake Road, a street where the more affluent residents of Skaneateles lived. Even as a teenager, Larry had lied to us about his true identity. We had no way of knowing that he had become a problem child. I doubt that Bill knew of Larry's criminal background either. But if he had, I do know Bill would have forgiven him and overlooked his past. Otherwise, Bill never would have allowed Larry into our home because Bill loved his family too much for that. If Bill had a major fault, it was that he was too quick to forgive and forget, and too willing to help anyone who asked him.

Bill was not a perfect person, as he himself would admit. No one is. But Bill was a good, honest man. He would give anyone the last dollar in his wallet or the sneakers off his feet, which is exactly what he did with the pair I gave him for his 19th birthday. He gave them to a homeless man who needed shoes. Bill was compassionate and non-judgmental. He cared about people and not about appearances. He looked for the good in everyone and believed there was good in everyone. Sometimes he would say, "You just have to look harder than usual at some folks." Bill loved life, and the world is lacking because of his death.

For this reason and many more, I pray constantly that God will give you the wisdom to use the power vested in you to sentence Larry Tutt to the most severe penalty allowable—life without parole. If Larry can do this to someone he grew up with and called his best friend, who will his next victim be? Please do not allow this man to put another family or person through what we will have to endure for the rest of our lives.

The last words Bill spoke to me were, "I love you, Mom. I'll see you." How little I knew that I would never see Bill's beautiful smile and loving face again until my days on earth are over.

Sincerely,

Beverly A. Freitag

If you would like to read more sample impact statements, visit
www.murdervictims.com and click on "victim impact statements."

Aftermath: In the Wake of Murder

ENDORSEMENTS

Carrie Freitag eloquently articulates the tragedy that the loved ones of homicide victims endure and at the same time offers an invaluable perspective on surviving such a tragedy. I recommend this book to any person who has lost a loved one by violence, professionals who work with crime victims, law enforcement, clergy, prosecutors, and any other criminal justice professionals.

—Dan Levey, President, Parents of Murdered Children, Inc.

Congratulations on expressing so much for so many so well! *Aftermath* provides an insightful view and much-needed validation of the feelings and torments of survivor grief after murder. All the thorny issues of rage, failure, guilt, forgiveness, and despair are candidly discussed, as well as the flaws of our criminal justice system. Bravo for the chapter, "The Old War On Terrorism," which puts murder in the U.S. in an updated and true perspective.

— Jean Lewis, Former President, Parents of Murdered Children, Inc.

A beautiful book. Readers will absolutely relate to the articulate and heartfelt writing. I applaud the author's willingness to dig deep into her own pain to reach out to others. *Aftermath* captures the true essence of loss and tragedy.

— Kimberly Goldman, VictimAdvocate

Aftermath is a bible on grief for the survivors of murder victims.

— Harry Hartman, Father of Ty Hartman (Murdered 11/9/98)

Aftermath is a book that will speak to the hearts of all homicide survivors. As the mother of a murdered daughter, I could relate to it all too well.

— Lois Duncan, Author of *Who Killed My Daughter* and *I Know What You Did Last Summer*

Aftermath maintains a sense of urgency. The writing is clear, accurate, and for the person who is in the sad position of "needing" this book, it will ring true. *Aftermath* is loaded with florid and colorful language that validates and gives permission to survivors to go out on the limb and start dealing with their issues and feelings. The chapter on rage primes the anger pump, gets it flowing, and then teaches how to mop it [the rage] up so no one slips in it and gets hurt.

— Sally VanOrman, MSW, CSW, Owner/Operator of The Womyns' Rooms A Retreat Home for Women, Ithaca, NY

More Titles From Chevron

Am I Alive? A Surviving Flight Attendant's Struggle and Inspiring Triumph Over Tragedy

Sandy Purl with Gregg Lewis

Sandy Purl fought for her life and the lives of her passengers when, 20 years ago, Southern Flight 242 went down in Georgia during a violent April hailstorm. And after the crash and her heroic efforts to aid the few survivors, she fought for her sanity. This story tells of one flight attendant's struggle with posttraumatic stress syndrome before resources were available in the airline industry to help survivors cope. Sandy tells the story of the crash and the history of critical incident stress management's entry into the aviation industry.

Building Self-Esteem: A 120-Day Program

Glenn R. Schiraldi

This is a guide to understanding and improving self-esteem for individuals, families, groups, and helpers. Readers learn essential skills and practice them in a systematic, step-by-step way until each skill is mastered. The volume is a vital resource for educators, mental health professionals, pastoral counselors, and paraprofessionals. Unique features include: clearly explained, skill-building exercises; a model for helping the person in distress; recommended reading list references; and ways to keep slips from turning into relapse.

Conquer Anxiety, Worry and Nervous Fatigue: A Guide to Great Peace

Glenn R. Schiraldi

This book focuses mainly on helping you understand and overcome the general worries, anxiety, and nervousness that can take the joy from your life and predispose you to anxiety disorders. You'll learn to recognize and understand the unusual symptoms. Step-by-step instructions guide you through proven strategies to conquer your symptoms. You'll be helped to develop your own program or to work with a mental health professional. Also discussed are causes of worry, anxiety, and nervous fatigue, the normal and natural courses of anxiety, and locating professional resources.

Falling Apart: Avoiding, Coping With, and Recovering From Stress Breakdown

Michael Epstein and Sue Hosking

Despite so many books being available on the general subject of stress, there are few that deal specifically with its serious consequences. Furthermore, no other comprehensive book on stress breakdown—the new and more appropriate term for the condition known as nervous breakdown—exists. Although it happens to ordinary people who appear to cope well with the usual demands of life, only those who have experienced stress breakdown know what it is like. Stories, private joys and agonies of those who have suffered from this debilitating experience are shared. *Falling Apart* shows you how to avoid stress breakdown, or how to cope with life if you or someone close to you has experienced a breakdown. This break-through book includes simple strategies for dealing with the many problems we encounter in today's stressful world and suggests ways to handle the dilemmas that confront those recovering from a breakdown.

For more information or to order on-line, visit our Web site at:

www.chevronpublishing.com

Or contact us at:
Chevron Publishing Corporation
5018 Dorsey Hall Drive, Suite 104 • Ellicott City, MD 21042 USA
(410) 740-0065 • office@chevronpublishing.com